GRAPHIC PRODUCTS

WITHDRAWN

Mike Finney

Head of Design and Technology,
William Farr CofE Comprehensive School, Welton

Contents

What is graphic products?

1·Industrial perspectives

INDUSTRIAL PERSPECTIVES 6

MANUFACTURING AND THE ECONOMY 7

SCALE OF PRODUCTION 9

GRAPHICS IN THE MANUFACTURING INDUSTRY 10

THE GRAPHICS INDUSTRY 12

MANUFACTURING PROCESSES 14

SAFETY 18

PUTTING IT INTO PRACTICE 20

2·Graphic techniques

GRAPHIC TECHNIQUES 21

CHOOSING MATERIALS — Griffen Paper Mill 22

MAKING YOUR MARK — Sanford UK 24

FREEHAND SKETCHING 26

3-DIMENSIONAL DRAWING 28

PERSPECTIVE DRAWING — CAD Associates 30

SHAPE AND FORM 34

USING COLOUR — Colin Plant, Graphic Designer 36

THE EFFECTS OF COLOUR 38

DRY MEDIA 40

WET MEDIA 41

HIGHLIGHTING IDEAS 42

WORKING WITH INK — Barking Dog Art 44

RENDERING 46

MARKERS 50

AIRBRUSHING 54

PHOTOGRAPHY 56

PRESENTING YOUR DRAWINGS 58

CADCAM — Castle Customs 60

PUTTING IT INTO PRACTICE 64

3·Geometrical and technical drawing

GEOMETRICAL AND TECHNICAL DRAWING   65
GEOMETRICAL AND TECHNICAL DRAWING continued   *Aesseal Plc*   66
LINES   68
DIMENSIONING   69
USING INFORMATION AND COMMUNICATION TECHNOLOGY   70
STANDARDISING DRAWINGS   72
ORTHOGRAPHIC PROJECTION   74
FIRST ANGLE PROJECTION   76
THIRD ANGLE PROJECTION   77
SECTIONS   78
ABBREVIATIONS AND CONVENTIONS   79
GEOMETRICAL DRAWING   80
CONSTRUCTIONS USING PLANE GEOMETRY   81
CONSTRUCTING SHAPES   82
PUTTING IT INTO PRACTICE   84

4·Modelling and prototyping

MODELLING AND PROTOTYPING   85
MODELLING AND PROTOTYPING continued   *Alan Miller Bunford*   86
SMART MATERIALS   90
MODELLING TOOLS   91
DEVELOPMENTS   *LINPAC*   92
FORMING   94
MOULDING   96
MODELLING WITH KITS   98
ADHESIVES   99
PUTTING IT INTO PRACTICE   100

5·Systems and control

SYSTEMS AND CONTROL 101
MECHANICAL SYSTEMS 102
USING MECHANISMS IN GRAPHIC PRODUCTS 104
ELECTRONIC SYSTEMS 106
BASIC ELECTRONIC COMPONENTS 107
PLANNING AND CONTROL 108
PUTTING IT INTO PRACTICE 110

6·Products and applications

PRODUCTS AND APPLICATIONS 111
PRODUCT DESIGN 112
INVESTIGATING EXISTING PRODUCTS 114
ENVIRONMENTAL ISSUES *Burton Waters* 116
ENVIRONMENTAL DESIGN *Burton Waters* 118
CORPORATE IMAGE DESIGN *English Rose Company* 122

Acknowledgements 126

Index 127

4

What is graphic products?

Graphic Products can be very difficult to define but the term is generally used to describe products whose primary function is to communicate information visually.

Graphic products are not new, they are as old as recorded history. Evidence of graphic products from the Stone Age still exists today on the walls of caves in France and Spain. Since then, graphic products have developed with art and illustration and have been influenced by design styles and fashion.

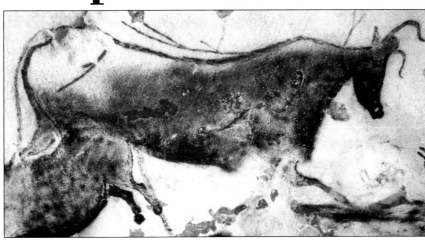

Cave paintings in Lascaux, France

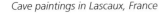

Early graphic products took the form of illuminated books which were produced by hand and combined text and graphics on the page. Graphic products, in the true sense, appeared in the mid-fifteenth century when Gutenberg began printing with metal blocks. In the sixteenth century Claude Garamond and others began to design type faces, some of which are still in use as computer fonts today. Little further progress was made until developments in printing machines in the nineteenth century allowed a whole new range of graphic products to be manufactured. The technological developments of the twentieth century had a significant effect on the development of Graphic Products and turned it into the hi-tech industry that it is today.

A page from the Gutenberg Bible

Industry employs a range of highly skilled graphic designers, illustrators, photographers and printers. They communicate with their audience through the use of words and images and produce graphic products in the form of posters, leaflets, brochures, magazines, newspapers, books, television images, websites as well as logos, corporate identities, advertising and packaging.

An early example of packaging

Graphic Products, as a subject in school, is the area of Design & Technology which relates broadly to the work undertaken by the graphic designers in industry.

It is about visual imagery and using compliant materials such as paper, card and plastics to solve problems and communicate 3-dimensional concepts to others. This includes designing and making such items as point of sale material, display stands, packaging, greetings cards, toys and games.

Examples of graphic products

5

1 · Industrial perspectives

The term 'industry' is often used to describe large manufacturing companies, such as multinational car companies. In reality, industry is much broader than this and includes all economic activities. Industry involves the whole process of manufacturing, trading and financial services. Industry produces **goods** and **services** which are offered to us, the consumers, to purchase.

Fig. 1.1 *The motor industry*

Industry is divided into three broad categories; primary, secondary, and tertiary. **Primary industries** are the industries concerned with the extraction of natural resources, for example, agriculture, fishing, forestry, mining and quarrying. **Secondary industries** are concerned with the manufacture and assembly of goods using the natural resources. These include food processing, packaging, electrical goods, electronic products, computers and cars. **Tertiary industries** are those companies involved in providing services. These include retailers (of clothes, food, etc.), banks, insurance companies, entertainment, health and education.

Fig. 1.2 *The 3 types of industry show how one business depends on another*

The development of industry in Britain began in the middle of the 18th century in the **Industrial Revolution**, with the early development of the steam engine and textiles manufacture. Factories replaced the smaller 'cottage' industries and then in the 19th century, new industries were created with the development of steel manufacture and the expansion of the railway system. By the end of the 19th century, new industries were opening up in many areas due to the development and expansion of electric power. The chemical industry and the motor industry, with its assembly-line production, developed in the early decades of the 20th century.

Industry is very important to the wealth creation of the country. A successful industrial nation is able to support a high standard of living by providing schools, hospitals, roads, railways and communication networks.

Fig. 1.3 *The Industrial Revolution created hardship for many, but made Great Britain the world's wealthiest nation*

6

MANUFACTURING AND THE ECONOMY

'Manufacturing continues to play an integral role in any growing and prosperous economy. UK manufacturing is in the midst of significant structural change. This in part reflects the inevitable implications of globalisation and the recognition that we should no longer be trying to compete on the basis of low cost, low value-added manufacturing, but rather through innovative, high technological products and processes.'
The Confederation of British Industry (CBI), December 2000

Fig. 1.4

The Confederation of British Industry (CBI) represents industry within the UK and the above statement, made at the very end of the 20th century, is very significant. Manufacturing industry within the UK has undergone many changes over the last forty years. In the 1960s and 70s the UK had a reputation for poor industrial relations, often resulting in strikes, and poor productivity (Fig. 1.5). **Productivity** is concerned with the profit that results from the investment made. Companies and shareholders invest in industry and they expect to profit from their investment. Poor productivity does not encourage people to invest. By becoming more efficient and focusing upon quality, good design and marketing, along with better industrial relations, UK industry has become world-class and attracted investment from around the world, this is good for the economy and for the country.

Fig. 1.6 *Hornby Hobbies, a long established British company now manufacturing overseas*

The CBI is saying here that there are more changes to be made and that much of this results from **globalisation**. Globalisation has happened through the use of ICT, the ability to communicate. It is as easy to communicate with a manufacturer or designer in another country as with people in another town. Companies have grown to be **multinational**.

Hornby Hobbies Ltd, for example are a long established British Company with a reputation for high quality products (Fig. 1.6). They have produced toys and models for many generations and continue to do so even though they no longer have a manufacturing base within

the UK. All Hornby model manufacture currently takes place in China.

Globalisation carries with it certain responsibilities. Some companies, particularly those who manufacture sports goods and clothing, have been criticised for exploiting poor countries by paying low wages and allowing poor working conditions. The companies argue that this is not knowingly the case and that they are in fact bringing much needed employment and investment to those countries. The manner by which the most industrialised nations bring about change in the developing world raises many important social issues.

Fig. 1.5 *Poor industrial relations like this are increasingly a thing of the past*

Fig. 1.7 *The Nissan car factory in Sunderland, a global Japanese company manufacturing in the UK for its European market*

7

MANUFACTURING IN THE UK

The UK manufacturing industry, which was historically based upon heavy industries, such as car manufacture, shipbuilding and iron and steel making, has reduced considerably in size over the period of great technological change, yet it remains vital to the economy.

Fig. 1.8 *A modern factory*

The UK creates 4% of the world's economy, this is called the **Gross Domestic Product (GDP)**, and 6 % of the worlds exports. This is from a nation with just 1% of the worlds population and a working population of 24 million people. Today manufacturing industry contributes around 20% of the UK GDP per year. Manufacturing also provides 4 million jobs directly and a further 4.5 million indirectly in support and services.

Manufacturing in the UK can be divided into **manufacturing sectors** in order to be able to see trends within a range of industries. The graph in Fig. 1.9 shows, over a two and a half year period, a comparison of output between a number of manufacturing sectors. The graph represents a trend and assumes that they started equal in 1995. The greatest fall in output can be seen to be the energy industries (coke, petroleum and nuclear) and the textiles, leather and clothing industries.

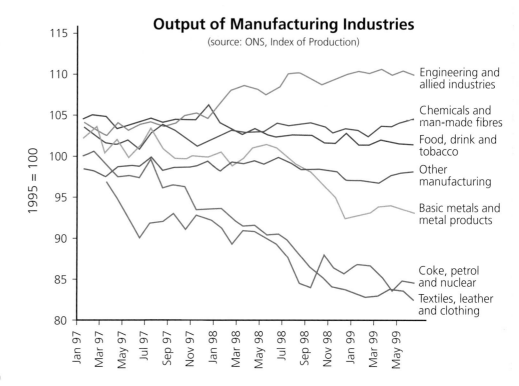

Fig. 1.9

Some UK manufacturing facts

The Automotive Industry
The UK is the home of 3 of the top 8 most productive car plants in Europe and 17 of the top 20 automotive component suppliers.

Aerospace Industries
The UK aerospace industry is the second largest in the world employing over 150 000 people and earning £17.5 billion.

The Food Industry
The UK food industry is the largest of all manufacturing sectors and contributes 13.5% of all manufacturing output. 460 000 people are employed in the food industry.

Technology Industries
The UK has the fifth largest electronics industry in the world employing 400 000 in manufacturing and 130 000 in software and software services.

The Pharmaceuticals Industry
The UK is the world's third largest exporter of pharmaceuticals and second to the USA in developing new medicines.

Biotechnology
The UK is the home of over 300 biotechnology companies and a further 460 related companies.

SCALE OF PRODUCTION

The term 'manufacturing' came into being in the eighteenth century, at the time of the Industrial Revolution. It refers to 'making' on a large or organised scale. For this reason the different types of manufacturing production are categorised according to their scale.

Process production

Process production, also known as **continuous production** is the name applied to those manufacturing processes that are continuous and only economic if they are kept running. This is true of many chemical and refining processes such as the production of fuel oils and gas. Aluminium, steel and many plastic materials are also manufactured on a continuous process. The cost of stopping and restarting the process production is greater than the cost of keeping the process operating. All forms of process production require high investment in capital equipment.

Mass Production

High volume, mass production is necessary for consumer products such as personal computers, cars and television sets in order to supply consumer demand at a low cost. This is also true of the standard components and sub-assemblies that these and many other products need, such as nuts, bolts, fastenings, springs, electrical components, batteries and paints.

Mass production, like process production, requires investment in specialist manufacturing equipment. This overall cost, however, is often balanced by low workforce costs and is located where labour is cheap. Mass production processes, particularly in assembly areas, consist of short easy to learn operations that are designed to gain maximum flexibility from a largely unskilled workforce.

Fig. 1.10 Process production

Fig. 1.11 Mass production

Fig. 1.12 Batch production

Fig. 1.13 Jobbing production

Batch production

A batch can be any specified quantity from a few to a few thousand. Batches or production runs can be repeated any number of times as required. The important feature of batch production is that the process, machines, tools and workforce are flexible. They must be able to change quickly from the production of a batch of one component to the production of another. Time spent changing over is known as down time. Down time is non-productive and expensive. It must therefore be kept to a minimum.

Batch production processes benefit from the flexibility of CNC machines, a skilled workforce and the adoption of modern manufacturing practices.

Jobbing production

Jobbing production, or **one-off production**, refers to the specialised processes involved in the manufacture of single items such as power stations, bridges, space craft and craft based products like jewellery and sculpture.

Jobbing production has a high unit cost and often requires highly skilled personnel.

It is important to recognise that industrial manufacturing is rarely as simple as this. In reality most manufacturing is a combination of these types of production. The key to economic, competitive manufacturing is often flexibility. Mass production processes are becoming increasingly flexible by introducing batch production cells within the mass production process. This still retains the low cost benefits of mass-production.

GRAPHICS IN THE MANUFACTURING INDUSTRY

In addition to forming an industry in its own right, graphics provides valuable support to the manufacturing industry at many levels, ranging from the design of the product through to manufacture, packaging, advertising, marketing and retailing. The graphics industry is explained on page 12.

Fig. 1.14 *Ideas sketch*

Design

Graphics are a communication tool used by most designers. Initial ideas are sketched. The sketches are used to communicate between the designers, the customer and the manufacturers. These sketches can take the form of simple rough sketches or they can be more elaborate presentation drawings. They are also likely to take the form of computer generated drawings and images, as computer aided design and illustration packages are increasingly used by designers.

Fig. 1.15 *A presentation drawing*

Fig. 1.16
Architectural drawing

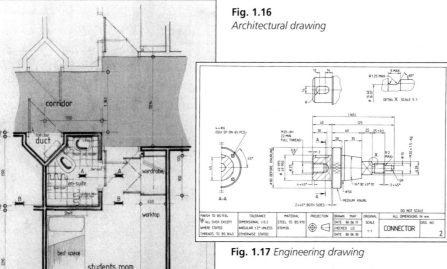

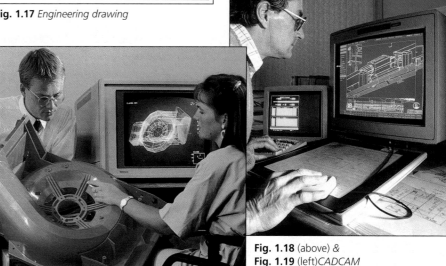

Fig. 1.17 *Engineering drawing*

Manufacturing

Graphics are also important in the manufacturing process where technical drawings are used to show how to make things. **Architectural drawings** and **engineering drawings** are typical examples of this. Graphics are also used to generate the **flow charts** and **production plans** used in manufacturing.

Computer aided design (CAD), drawings and 3-dimensional models are used to generate the data from which computer controlled machines are able to manufacture products and components. This process of using CAD to control the whole of the manufacturing process is known as **CIM** or **computer integrated manufacture**.

Fig. 1.18 (above) &
Fig. 1.19 (left)*CADCAM*

Packaging

Graphics are extensively used in the design of packaging. Finished package designs provide us with excellent examples of Graphic Products. The function of packaging is to communicate visual information about a number of things including the contents, manufacturers and product information etc. It also protects the goods inside from damage until they are required for use.

Fig. 1.20 *Examples of packaging*

Advertising and marketing

The advertising industry relies almost entirely on graphics, in one form or another, to communicate its message. Visual images are extremely important and logos are used to create images for both companies and products. This is particularly important in TV and internet advertising where it can be used to create or increase the demand for products and services. Like packaging, advertising and marketing provide a rich source of graphic products.

Fig. 1.21 *Examples of company logos*

Retailing

Graphics are important in retailing and are used to create window displays, exhibitions, point of sale material, brochures and catalogues. Modern retailing relies very much on graphics and incorporates the product's visual images into advertising campaigns, packages and point of sale material.

Fig. 1.22 *Graphic products in a supermarket*

Several large manufacturing companies have retailed other products which incorporate their logos and product images. Caterpillar is an example of this. An established company, well known for making earth-moving equipment, it now licenses a range of clothing and other goods aimed at young people. Like packaging and advertising, retailing provides many examples of graphic products.

Fig. 1.23 *Caterpillar products*

11

THE GRAPHICS INDUSTRY

The graphics industry consists of printing, packaging and graphic communications companies and is the **UK's fifth largest manufacturing industry**. It employs around **170 000 people** in more than **12 000 companies** which manufacture products such as advertising material, publications, packaging and stationery. The industry is made up of small companies rather than large multi-national organisations, with just 20 companies employing more than 400 people and approximately 575 employing between 50 and 399 people. These companies tend to specialise in a narrow range of products in national and international markets. There are a vast number of small firms, around 12 000, which cater for local markets, but account for more than half of the industry's sales.

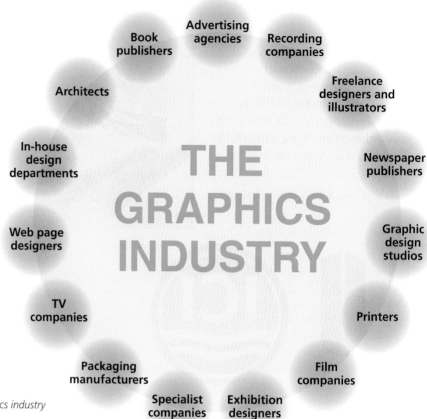

Fig. 1.24 *Contributors to the graphics industry*

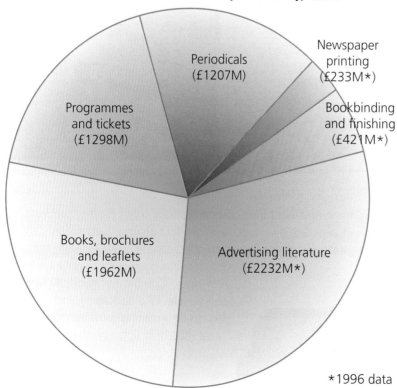

UK Manufacturer Sales (Prodcom), 1997

Fig. 1.25 *UK sales of graphic products*

Net capital expenditure in the graphics industry in recent years has been around £750 million annually.

The value of sales is about £13 billion, 1.7% of UK gross domestic product.

The industry makes a positive contribution to the trade balance. Exports of graphic products are dominated by publications and periodicals. The balance of trade in printed products improved between 1990 and 1997, from £141 million to £712 million, before falling to £548 million in 1998 because of the strength of sterling.

The graphics industry serves all parts of the economy: central and local government, financial services, retailing, distribution, travel and tourism and the manufacturing industry.

As a nation we spend approximately £215 for every man, woman and child on printed products, packaging and stationery every year.

12

Graphic designers in industry

Graphic designers today work in many areas ranging from the more traditional graphic products, such as advertising materials, packaging, brochures and posters, to maps, books, coins, stamps, phonecards and banknotes. Graphic designers are also employed in other fields including ceramics, textiles, sign making and websites for the internet.

Fig. 1.26 *Examples of graphic products*

The graphic design process

Commissioning

Designer & client discuss the brief and draw up a specification

↓

Roughs

Designer produces roughs of possible designs

↓

Client Approval

Roughs are discussed with client and the final design agreed

↓

Costings

Costings and schedules are discussed and agreed with the client

↓

Paste Up

Designer brings together illustrations, photographs and text to produce paste up in either artwork or DTP form

↓

Production

The printer receives the paste up, makes the printing plates and produces a proof copy for checking before the final print run is made.

Fig. 1.27 *The graphic design process*

Graphic designs go through several different stages before the final graphic product is produced. These stages may vary slightly according to the nature of the work. The process is generally very similar to the stages that you will work through in your project work.

Commissioning is normally the first stage. The most suitable designer is chosen to undertake the work. A briefing meeting takes place between the client and the designer. Design details are discussed and the designer draws up a specification based on the client's requirements.

The designer will then produce initial ideas of his designs. These roughs, as they are known, will either be in the form of sketches and marker drawings or computer generated designs. Many designers still prefer to produce roughs by hand and develop them later using computer graphics software.

The designer will be expected to provide the client with estimates of the costs of the project and details of the time schedule. He or she will need to take into account the cost of photographs and illustrations that may be required as well as the printing costs.

When the client is happy with the design and the estimated costs, the designer will go ahead and prepare the final artwork for printing. This final stage is known as the **paste up** stage. It used to involve actually cutting and pasting the illustrations and text together to form the final design. Nowadays it can all be done using computers and desktop publishing software (DTP). At the paste up stage, the design details are finalised and the printing instructions specified. The paste up is then sent to the printer, either in the form of artwork or as a computer file. The graphics industry uses a common file format known as a **JPEG** (Joint photographics expert group). The printer will set up the page, make the printing plate and then print off a **proof copy** for the designer and the client to approve before the final printing begins.

MANUFACTURING PROCESSES

The nature of graphic products varies considerably from printed material through to plastics mouldings, metal cans, boxes and ceramic ware. As a result of this a range of different manufacturing processes are employed by industry.

Printing

Printing is the most important manufacturing process used in the making of a graphic product. A number of methods, including gravure and flexography are used, but **offset lithography** and **screen printing** are still the most common forms of commercial printing.

Fig. 1.28 *An early printing press*

Offset lithography

The basic principle of lithography is that oil and water do not mix. The process was developed in 1798 in Germany by Aloys Senefelder, who found that if a drawing were made on a flat piece of limestone with a greasy crayon, the lines would hold an oil based ink when the stone was wet. The other parts of the stone would take no ink and a drawing could be made by rolling a piece of paper onto the stone. Modern litho printing plates have non-image areas which absorb water. During printing the plate is kept wet so that the ink, which is oily, is rejected by the wet areas and stays on the image areas.

Fig. 1.29 *Printing with a modern offset litho machine*

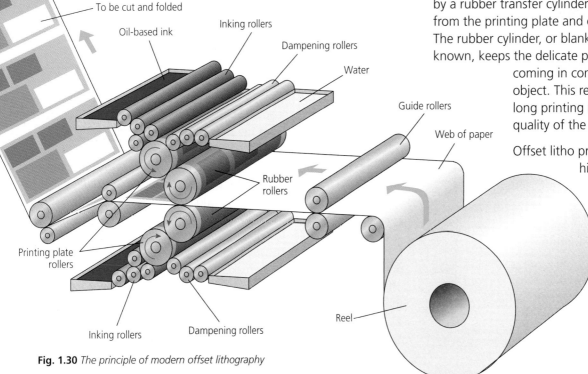

To be cut and folded
Oil-based ink
Inking rollers
Dampening rollers
Water
Guide rollers
Web of paper
Rubber rollers
Printing plate rollers
Inking rollers
Dampening rollers
Reel

The flat piece of limestone has now been replaced by a rubber transfer cylinder which takes the image from the printing plate and offsets it onto the paper. The rubber cylinder, or blanket as it is sometimes known, keeps the delicate printing plate from coming in contact with the printed object. This reduces wear and allows long printing runs without losing the quality of the reproduction.

Offset litho printing is used where high volume printing is required such as in the making of newspapers. The diagram on the left shows how the process works in a typical web offset litho machine.

Fig. 1.30 *The principle of modern offset lithography*

Four-colour process printing

The majority of graphic products are printed in full colour using the four-colour process. The artwork is separated to produce four printing plates, one for each of the four ink colours. The ink colours, Cyan (Blue), Magenta (Red), Yellow and Black, are often referred to as **CMYK**. The inks used are translucent and can be overprinted and combined in a variety of different proportions to produce a wide range of colours. Each piece of work is printed four times in order to produce the full colour effect.

cyan

magenta

yellow

black

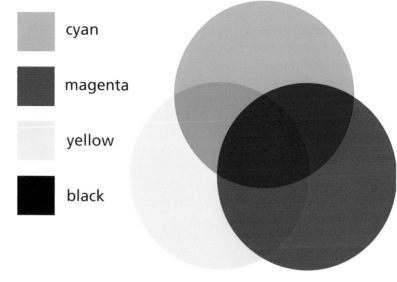

Fig. 1.32 shows the four printing plates required to print the full coloured picture on the right.

Fig. 1.31 *The process colours*

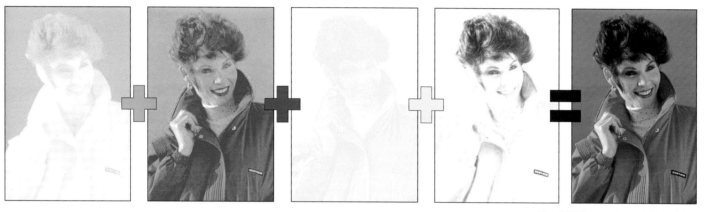

Fig. 1.32 *Four-colour printing plates*

Screen printing

Fig. 1.33 *Screen printing*

In screen printing, the ink is transferred to the printing surface by being squeezed through a fine fabric sheet or metal mesh stretched on a frame. Originally, the screens used were made of silk. The screen carries a stencil which defines the image area. The process can be manual or mechanical but is most suitable for short runs. Screen printing is used for large poster work, display material and fabrics such as T-shirts. It comes into its own when printing onto difficult or unusual surfaces such as clothing or plastic objects. This process is used to print the design on drinks cans and similar metal packaging.

This process is still sometimes referred to as silkscreen printing, although the screens are generally made from artificial fibres today rather than silk.

Plastics and plastics manufacturing processes are very important in Graphic Products. The properties of plastics make them an invaluable material for processing, storing, transporting, protecting and preserving products. In the UK, 36% of plastics are used in the manufacture of packaging. Designers need to understand the manufacturing processes that will be used to manufacture their designs. One of the most common manufacturing processes used in packaging is **thermoforming**. This is when thermoplastic material is heated and formed into items which will contain products and protect them until they are required for use.

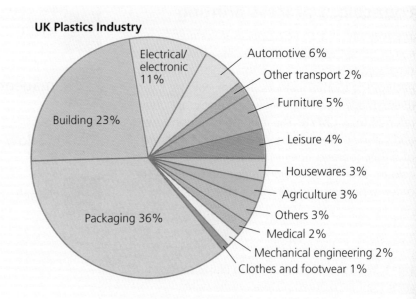

UK Plastics Industry

Building 23%
Electrical/electronic 11%
Packaging 36%
Automotive 6%
Other transport 2%
Furniture 5%
Leisure 4%
Housewares 3%
Agriculture 3%
Others 3%
Medical 2%
Mechanical engineering 2%
Clothes and footwear 1%

Fig. 1.34 *Plastic applications in the UK*

Vacuum forming

One of the most widely used thermoforming processes is vacuum forming. In this process, hot thermoplastic sheets such as **high impact polystyrene** or **ABS** are draped over a mould. Air is removed from between the mould and the hot plastic. This creates a vacuum that draws the plastic down into the cavities of the mould. When the plastic cools, the thermoplastic sheet retains the shape of the mould and the moulded product can be removed.

Vacuum forming moulds are made from a variety of different materials: wood, clay, plaster, epoxy resin or aluminium.

Wood or MDF is commonly used in schools as it is easy to work with, readily available and can produce high quality vacuum formed products.

Fig. 1.35 *An industrial vacuum forming machine*

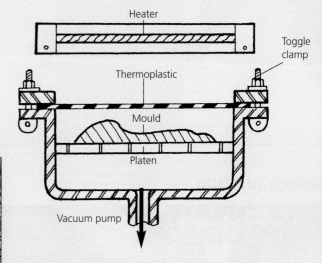

Heater
Toggle clamp
Thermoplastic
Mould
Platen
Vacuum pump

Fig. 1.36 *Diagram of a vacuum forming machine*

The mould surface should be dry and free from dust particles. When using MDF, a sealant such as polyurethane varnish or shellac should be applied to the mould in order to prevent dust particles from getting into the vacuum pump.

During cooling, the thermoplastic material shrinks tight around the mould and can be difficult to remove. To prevent this, it is necessary to put a slight angle on the vertical parts of the mould. This is called a draft angle and should be a minimum of five degrees.

Fig. 1.37 *Vacuum forming used in packaging*

16

Blow moulding

Blow moulding is the process used to manufacture plastic bottles and containers. **High density polyethylene** (HDPE) and **low density polyethylene** (LDPE) are both used for blow moulding as are other types of thermoplastics. A length of plastic, known as a **parison** is extruded in between two halves of a mould. The mould closes and air is blown into the parison shaping it into the form of the mould.

After the moulding is ejected, the excess plastic or 'flash' is removed using a rotary cutter. The container is then decorated by either silk screen printing or the application of pre-printed paper labels.

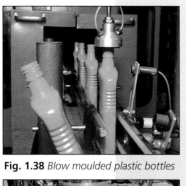

Fig. 1.38 *Blow moulded plastic bottles*

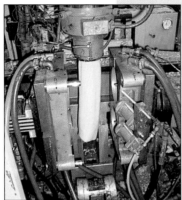

Fig. 1.39 *A blow moulding machine showing the extruded parison*

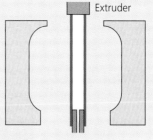

1. The parison is extruded in between the two halves of the mould.

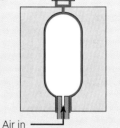

2. The mould closes and the parison is inflated.

Air in

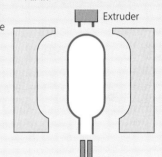

3. The mould opens and the blown shape is ejected.

Fig. 1.40 *The blow moulding process*

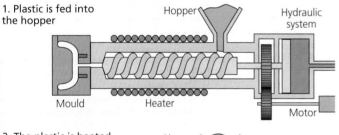

1. Plastic is fed into the hopper

Hopper · Hydraulic system · Mould · Heater · Motor

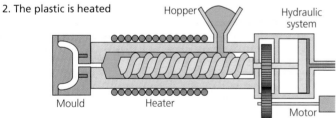

2. The plastic is heated

Hopper · Hydraulic system · Mould · Heater · Motor

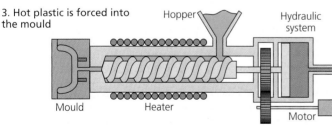

3. Hot plastic is forced into the mould

Hopper · Hydraulic system · Mould · Heater · Motor

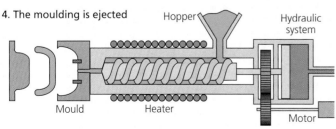

4. The moulding is ejected

Hopper · Hydraulic system · Mould · Heater · Motor

Fig. 1.43 *The injection moulding process*

Injection moulding

Injection moulding is a more complicated and expensive process than blow moulding. It is a highly automated manufacturing process used for producing large numbers of identical products. Granulated or powdered thermoplastic material is heated, melted and then forced under pressure into a mould. The plastics material cools and the component takes the shape of the mould cavity.

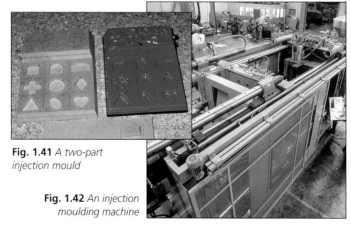

Fig. 1.41 *A two-part injection mould*

Fig. 1.42 *An injection moulding machine*

A large number of plastic products are manufactured using the injection moulding process. These include buckets, washing up bowls and computer cases, in addition to a number of containers used in packaging.

SAFETY

Safety is extremely important at all levels in graphic products, from the design of the products themselves to the materials and manufacturing processes used to make them. Safety is the responsibility of everyone, from designers to machine operators.

Product Safety

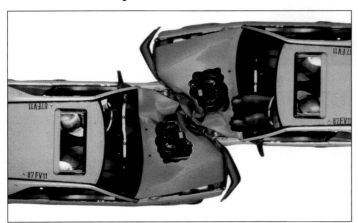

Designers have a responsibility for their products and can be held legally responsible for injury caused by them. They must be safe and not harm the user. Much has been done in recent years to make the products we use safer. A considerable amount of research now goes into both the materials to be used and the actual products. This can be clearly seen in the motor industry where cars are now designed to protect the occupants in the event of an accident. Cars are now tested and have to meet strict safety standards before they can be sold.

Fig. 1.44 *An aerial view of crash testing*

Safety in industry

The safety of people working in industry is controlled by an Act of Parliament. The **Health and Safety at Work Act** of 1974 was introduced to make the workplace safer for employees and help to reduce some of the time lost due to illness and injury. Health and Safety regulations cover a wide field, ranging from ventilation and temperature to noise levels and protective clothing. Health and Safety Inspectors have the right to enter premises and take measurements, photographs and samples as part of an investigation. Employers can be found at fault if the relevant procedures have not been followed.

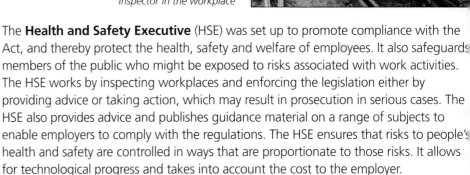

Fig. 1.45 *A Health and Safety inspector in the workplace*

Fig. 1.46 *The HSE logo*

The **Health and Safety Executive** (HSE) was set up to promote compliance with the Act, and thereby protect the health, safety and welfare of employees. It also safeguards members of the public who might be exposed to risks associated with work activities. The HSE works by inspecting workplaces and enforcing the legislation either by providing advice or taking action, which may result in prosecution in serious cases. The HSE also provides advice and publishes guidance material on a range of subjects to enable employers to comply with the regulations. The HSE ensures that risks to people's health and safety are controlled in ways that are proportionate to those risks. It allows for technological progress and takes into account the cost to the employer.

The **Control of Substances Hazardous to Health (COSHH)** regulations of 1988 were introduced to protect people from the effects of materials, substances and processes used in their work. Long-term exposure to some of these can cause long-term effects to health and, in some cases, serious illness. The COSHH regulations require that levels of hazardous substances be kept below certain levels. Some substances are subject to a **Maximum Exposure Limit** (MEL) and employers must ensure that contact with the substance is kept below this limit. Other substances are subject to an **Occupational Exposure Standard** (OES) which must not be exceeded except for a temporary situation where the employer is taking steps to remedy the situation.

Risk assessment

Materials and processes used must be analysed to determine any effect they may have on the user. Information is then made available, consisting of the identification of the hazards, assessments of the risks and the measures that need to be taken to control them.

A risk assessment sheet should be available for any process or material determined as being a hazard in your school workshops. A risk assessment sheet for acrylic cement is shown on the right.

Fig. 1.47 *A risk assessment sheet*

Safety at school

The Health and Safety regulations also apply to school workshops and you are expected to comply with a code of practice known as British Standard 4163. You must always think about your own safety and that of others – one brief lapse of concentration could result in an accident that could change your life or someone else's forever. **Always follow instructions and safety rules carefully**.

Fig. 1.48 *The safety check symbol*

This safety symbol is used throughout the book to draw your attention to potential hazards and warnings you need to heed, relating to safety.

Fig. 1.49 *Safety symbols – be aware of them.*

ADHESIVES	Applicable to:	See also:
ACRYLIC CEMENT	acrylic cement e.g. Tensol	

Process: Spreading cement on joint surfaces; pouring from a large stock container to smaller ones. Cement contains methyl methacrylate in a solvent, usually methylene chloride or trichloroethylene (which are both non-flammable).

HAZARDS

Toxic — Hazardous by inhalation and by swallowing.
Irritant — Irritating to the skin, eyes and respiratory tract.
Flammable — If a flammable solvent is used, flammable or explosive vapour-air mixtures may form. Thermal decomposition will evolve toxic and flammable vapours.

RISK ASSESSMENT

Toxic — Methylene chloride (dichloromethane): MEL is 100 parts per million (8h TWA)[1] or 250 parts per million (10 min ref period) (under review). Trichloroethylene (trichloroethene): MEL is 100 parts per million (8h TWA) or 150 parts per million (10 min ref period). In school workshop activities, the 8 h hazard levels will be reached only in the event of a major spill or use in a small, unventilated room. The 10 min hazard levels will not be exceeded if the total area of exposed adhesive is less than 500cm².

Irritant — Cement splashes must be kept out of eyes and off sensitive skin.
Flammable — Vapour from some solvents could be ignited by flames or red-hot metal

CONTROL MEASURES

If containers are opened and used only in well-ventilated areas, local exhaust ventilation will not be required for normal use.

If the 10 min hazard level might be exceeded, either local exhaust ventilation must be provided (with regular examination) or an HSE-approved respirator must be worn (subject to 3-month inspection)

Eye protection must be worn. Gloves are advisable for sensitive skin

The work must be at least 1m from source of ignition.

Disposal — Collect solids for disposal in accordance with local regulations
Storage — Keep containers tightly closed in a cool well-ventilated place where there should be no smoking

---

How to behave

- Behave sensibly at all times. Do not run, shout, fool about or distract others.
- Move around and carry tools and materials in a safe manner.

What to wear

- Before starting work with any tools or equipment, remove or tuck in ties, take off jewellery and tie back long hair.
- Wear aprons or overalls to protect clothes, as well as stout shoes.
- Wear special protective clothing and eye protection when required.
- Always wear the safety items provided for you and make sure they are put back for others to use.

What to do

- Keep your work area well organised, clean and tidy.
- Keep both hands behind the cutting edge when using sharp tools.
- Clean and return all equipment to its proper place. Report any faults, damage or breakages.
- Always read the instructions on chemically based products such as glues or solvents. Only use them in a safe, well ventilated area.
- Avoid inhaling large amounts of dust – wear a face mask when using sanders.
- Clean up and wash your hands after work.

19

Putting it into practice

1 **a** What do you understand by the term *industry*?

  b Explain why industry is important to the nation as a whole.

2 Explain what is meant by *primary*, *secondary* and *tertiary industries*. Give examples.

3 What is meant by the term *mixed economy*?

4 Explain what is meant by *manufacturing*.

5 Explain, with examples, what is meant by *job production*.

6 Explain, with examples what is meant by *batch production*.

7 Describe how computer aided design is used in the graphics industry.

8 Explain what is meant by the term *CIM*.

9 Draw a diagram to show the many trades or disciplines which contribute to the graphics industry.

10 Explain the differences between a freelance graphic designer and an in-house graphic designer.

11 Find out as much as you can about the development of graphic products in the nineteenth century.

12 Choose a familiar graphic product and trace its progress through the graphic design process.

13 Describe the modern offset lithography process. Use sketches and diagrams to illustrate your answer.

14 Describe the screen printing process and give examples of graphic products printed using this process.

15 Name the colours used in the CMYK process.

16 With the aid of coloured diagrams, describe how four colour process printing is carried out.

17 Describe the process of vacuum forming and, with the aid of examples, explain how it is used in graphic products.

18 Describe the process of blow moulding and give examples of its use in the graphics industry.

19 Make a diagram to show the sequence of operations used in the process of injection moulding a simple container.

20 Explain why safety is important in all aspects of graphic products and describe the role of the Health and Safety Executive.

2 · Graphic techniques

Good graphic skills are essential requirements for this subject. This section will help you to develop the graphic techniques necessary for a GCSE course in Graphic Products.

In the same way that professional graphic designers need to be able to produce roughs of their ideas to show to clients, you also need to be able to communicate your ideas clearly. You do not need to be an artist to be able to communicate your design ideas. This section shows you how to develop your skills to produce quality design work.

Fig. 2.1 *A student and a designer at work*

The section begins by looking at basic techniques and provides opportunities for you to develop your 3-dimensional sketching skills. The exercises included are intended for you to work through on your own, so you can develop the skills you need for the subject.

The section also covers the techniques required for you to develop and present your ideas. Light and shade, using colour, rendering and presentation techniques are all included to help you use your graphic skills to communicate your design ideas.

Fig. 2.2 *(Above) Examples of a designer's sketches of ideas for a juice carton*

By the time you have completed the section you will be able to use a number of graphic techniques to communicate your design ideas clearly. With practice, you will be able to confidently produce design ideas, roughs or visuals to use in your project work.

Fig. 2.3 *Finished ideas*

Michael Gibbs, at Griffen Paper Mill in the southwest of England, is one of the few people left in Britain who manufacture paper by hand. The market for handmade paper is very specialised, and Griffen Paper Mill has identified a 'market niche' in the repair of ancient books and documents. Bookbinders and the British Library are amongst the mill's customers – and one of its recent tasks was making paper for repairing pages in a very old book for Canterbury Cathedral.

The process that Michael follows is similar to that used up until the end of the eighteenth century. The mill buys in waste textile fibres and Michael beats them into paper pulp using a 'Hollander' beater (a machine which was invented during the seventeenth century). These fibres are transferred to a vat and mixed with water to form the paper pulp. Then a paper mould (a fine wire mesh on a wooden frame) is dipped into the vat. When the mould is lifted out, a layer of pulp has collected on the top, which, once the water has drained from it, forms the sheet of paper.

CHOOSING MATERIALS

The materials and equipment that you choose to work with when you are designing will depend very much on what you want to do and how far ahead you are with your design. Different materials and equipment are needed at each stage of your work. For instance, when you first start forming ideas you will want to work with materials that will allow you to work quickly, whereas at the working-drawing stage you will need to use materials which enable you to be very precise and show exactly how you intend to realise your design.

Fig. 2.4 *Choose the right tools for the job*

Get the right support

Drawing surfaces such as paper and card are sometimes called 'supports'. It is very important to use the correct support for the type of drawing you are doing and for the medium that you have chosen to work with. Soft pencils work best on a rough surface; inks and markers require a paper or board which will not allow them to run or bleed; and wet media such as gouache and watercolours need a specially prepared surface which will not wrinkle when water is applied.

Fig. 2.5 *It is important to choose the right support for the job*

Papers and boards

There is an enormous selection of papers and boards available, ranging from newsprint (paper for newspapers) and layout paper to high-quality illustration board and expensive heavy watercolour paper.

Paper is described by its size, weight and texture. You have probably noticed the letters A3 or A4 on sketchbooks or notepads.

The newly formed sheets are then 'couched' (laid down) between layers of felt and pressed to remove any remaining water. After pressing, the sheets and felts are separated and the paper is dried.

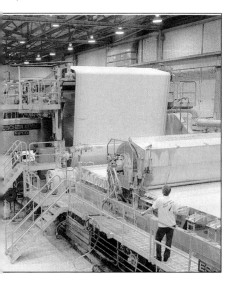

Of course, this is not an ideal method for producing paper in the quantity that we use today! Now there are machines that use much the same process, but produce paper automatically and on a much larger scale. (The first practical paper-making machines were introduced around 1800, and machines in use today use the same principles.)

There are two main types of paper-making machine:

1 Cylinder mould machines, which are used to produce high-quality watercolour papers like the ones you use in school.
2 Foudrinier machines (like the one shown here), which are faster than cylinder mould machines but cannot produce such high-quality paper. Most mass-produced paper (like the paper for this book) is produced on this type of machine.

These letters and numbers refer to the international standard paper sizing system, in which an A0 sheet of paper has an area of 1 square metre. A sheet of A1 paper (594 × 841 mm) is half the size of an A0 sheet. The next size down is A2 which is exactly half the size of A1. A3 is half the size of A2, and so on, down to A6. The diagram in Fig. 2.6 will help you to understand the sizing system. You will probably find that A3 paper is the most convenient size for most of your work.

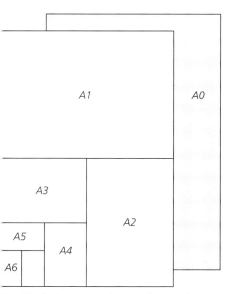

Fig. 2.6 *The international standard paper sizes*

Watch your weight

The thickness and density of a sheet of paper is usually described by its *weight*. For example, the paper used in a photocopier normally has a weight of about 80 gsm. The letters 'gsm' stand for 'grammes per square metre'. Ordinary watercolour paper has a weight of 300 gsm. In other words, an A0 size sheet of this paper actually weighs 300 grammes, and a single A2 sheet weighs 75 grammes. If you compare the thickness of the two types of paper you will see that a sheet of watercolour paper is much thicker than a sheet of copier paper. The thicker the paper the more it weighs. The pages of this book are made from 105 gsm paper. The size of each page is A4. What do you think the weight of each page is?

The rough and the smooth

It is also very important to consider the texture of the paper that you use in your design work. The roughness of the paper surface is known as the 'tooth', and it is determined by the way the paper is made. There are three types of paper surfaces available: hot pressed (HP), cold pressed (CP) and rough. Hot-pressed paper has a smooth surface with very little tooth, making it ideal for use with pencils, pens, ink and washes. Cold-pressed paper has a rougher surface and is suitable for drawing with chalk, soft-leaded pencils and gouache. Rough paper has a textured surface which is very good for working in watercolour and for work where paint, ink and pencil are mixed. Good quality papers can be really expensive, but a high-standard cartridge paper with a weight of about 120 gsm will be suitable for most of your work.

Fig. 2.7 *There are many different textures of paper available.*

Berol is one of Sanford UK's leading brand names in pens and pencils. Based in King's Lynn, Sanford UK is a company which manufactures and distributes writing instruments and artists' materials. Its products are exported to at least 98 countries, even Japan, where some of it's major competitors are based.

Berol logo

Although we do not know when the first pencil was invented, Conrad Gesner, a Swiss naturalist, described his 'writing rod held in a wooden case' in his book Treatise on Fossils, *published in 1565. There have been a number of variations since that time. Today, the pencil industry is an international business, using raw materials from every corner of the globe.*

The pencil 'leads' are made of a mixture of graphite (a natural mineral similar to coal) and clay, finely ground, thoroughly mixed, and fired in ovens to produce a strong fused stick, similar to chinaware. Sanford UK use amorphous graphite from Mexico in the manufacture of their pencils. Sanford UK's invention, the 'attrition mill', blows two jets of highly compressed air, containing graphite particles, directly at each other, enabling the particles of graphite to grind themselves into powder.

The clay, which comes mainly from Bavaria, is mixed with water and refined to remove all grit and heavier elements, leaving only the finest microscopic particles to be mixed with the graphite.

MAKING YOUR MARK

Charcoal

Fig. 2.8 *Charcoal comes in a wide range of pencils and sticks*

Charcoal is made out of wood (usually willow or vine twigs) which has been deliberately and carefully burnt. It has been used as a drawing material for centuries. You can buy charcoal today in either stick form or pencil form. It is very effective for communicating design because it allows you to work quickly to show the general outlines of your ideas. It is ideal for sketching on a large scale and is an excellent material for shading. You will not be able to show the fine details of your design with charcoal, but it is excellent for giving general impressions.

When you use charcoal you should take care, as it smudges very easily. However, this can at times be used to advantage, and charcoal work is often deliberately smudged to create tonal effects. To prevent your finished charcoal drawings smudging and making a mess of your folder, they need to be fixed. This involves spraying the drawing with a fixative spray which seals the surface of the work so that it cannot be accidentally smudged. Take care when using fixative sprays. Always use them in a well-ventilated area or a special spray booth.

Pencils

Pencils are the most commonly used drawing instrument and they are available in a wide variety of types and styles. You can buy up to 19 different grades of traditional graphite pencil. They are graded according to their degree of hardness. The letter H is used to indicate the harder pencils and B is used to denote the softer ones. Soft pencils produce a black line while the harder types produce a grey one.

The softest grade, 8B, is used mainly by artists, while the hardest grade, 9H, is often used by stonemasons.

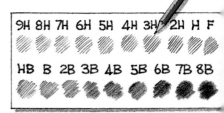

Fig. 2.9 *The range of graphite pencil grades*

Clutch and fine-lead pencils

Many people prefer to use clutch pencils and fine-lead pencils. These have plastic barrels, rather like ball pens, with a push-button mechanism which feeds the lead out of the tip, ready for drawing. Clutch pencils have their own sharpener built into the pencil, whereas fine-lead pencils have leads which are so fine that they never need sharpening. Both types of pencil use graphite and polymer leads which, like traditional graphite pencils, are available in varying degrees of hardness.

The graphite and clay are then mixed together in varying proportions. It is these proportions that determine the degree of hardness of the pencil. The more graphite that is used in the mixture, the softer and blacker the pencil will be.

The casing for the 'lead' is made from Californian cedar wood. The wood is first sawn into slats, each six or seven pencils wide. It is then seasoned, and run through a grooving machine. The grooves are impregnated with a resinous binding material that locks the wood fibres and stops them splitting. The graphite/clay sticks are then laid in the grooves. Glue is applied to a second slat, which is similarly grooved, and the two slats are pressed together to form a sandwich. These 'sandwiches' are washed, thoroughly dried, and fed into a moulding machine which forms them into individual pencils. Following the application of several coats of lacquer, they are hot-foil stamped with the brand name and grade before they are sharpened.

Every pencil is rigorously inspected. Laboratory staff sample and check their quality to ensure a perfect finished product, both in appearance and performance.

Making your point

Keeping a sharp point on your pencil is very important, especially if your drawings have to be accurate and show precise details. Most pencils can be sharpened using a bench-mounted rotary machine or a small pocket-sized sharpener. Soft pencils are best sharpened with a sharp knife blade, as the points can break in conventional sharpeners.

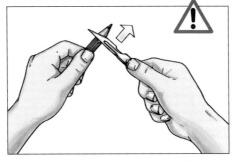

Fig. 2.11 *Sharpening a pencil with a knife*

Always take care when using knives – hold the pencil firmly in one hand and cut away from your body. Cut with a slicing action and rotate the pencil after each cut in order to make an even point. After sharpening a pencil with a knife, it is a good idea to use a piece of glass paper to make a really sharp point.

Ball pens

Ball pens are very useful for making quick sketches and recording ideas as they come to you. They were originally thought of in the late 1890s but the product was not patented until 1937. Since then, they have been developed into versatile and inexpensive writing instruments.

They require very little care and maintenance and will successfully make marks on a wide range of papers and boards. The ball pen is so-called because its tip consists of a ball housed in a socket. The ball transfers a special quick-drying ink from an inner plastic tube on to the paper. There is a vast range of ball pens available in a variety of ink colours and in several different line widths. They can be used for line work, texture and shading.

Fig. 2.12 *You can buy a range of ball pens in the shops.*

The use of other drawing instruments, such as coloured pencils and felt-tip pens will be explored in the next chapter.

Fig. 2.10 *Clutch and fine-lead pencils*

FREEHAND SKETCHING

The most suitable form of drawing for generating and recording ideas is freehand sketching. This type of drawing is done without the help of drawing aids such as a ruler or a pair of compasses. You need to record your ideas as quickly as possible before you forget them – using a ruler would slow down this process and break up the flow of ideas. Good freehand sketches are lively and interesting, and provide a record of your thinking process.

Ideas can be explained in a sketch more easily than in words. Sketches are very effective in communicating your ideas to other people, but more importantly at this stage in the design process, they enable you to visualise your own ideas more clearly and help you to go on and develop them.

Freehand sketches can be made using any medium that allows you to work quickly. Pencil, fine-line marker pen, charcoal and ball pen are all suitable. You should use whatever equipment you are most comfortable with. Sketches can be made on a wide variety of surfaces. Some people prefer to work on cartridge paper, but many designers work on layout paper which can be overlaid and traced through, in case an idea needs to be developed or redrawn. Drawing well and communicating fluently using graphics media takes time, so don't worry if your drawings don't look like the one in Fig. 2.13 to begin with. Remember that everyone can draw – it just takes a little practice to be good at it.

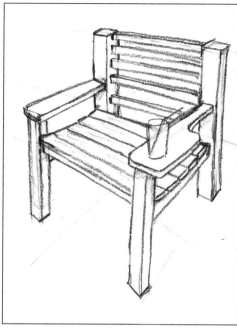

Fig. 2.13 A designer's freehand sketch

Sketching exercises – Try working through the following exercises to help you develop your freehand sketching skills.

1 Begin by holding your pen or pencil lightly between your thumb and first finger. Hold your hand so that it can move easily across the paper and freely in all directions. Don't plant your hand on the paper and draw by only moving your fingers – move your whole hand.

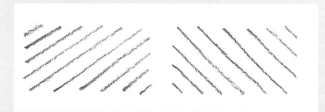

Fig. 2.14 Holding the pencil correctly will help you sketch more easily

3 Now try drawing horizontal lines. Draw the lines approximately 75 mm long, keeping them as straight as possible (without using a ruler). Remember to draw by moving your arm across the paper, using your little finger as a support if necessary. Try doing the same thing with vertical lines. (Don't cheat by turning the paper around.)

Fig. 2.16 Vertical and horizontal lines

2 Now try drawing lines. Start by drawing diagonal lines like the ones in Fig. 2.15. Diagonal lines are the easiest to draw naturally – try drawing both ways and see which you find easier. Let your hand move freely across the page. Draw quickly, and don't worry if the lines are not straight – it doesn't matter at this stage.

Fig. 2.15 Diagonal lines

4 To develop your pencil control further, draw two dots about l00 mm apart and then join them with your pencil, as shown in Fig. 2.17. Repeat this exercise at least 10 times and then try the same thing with vertical lines.

Fig. 2.17 Using dots to draw horizontal lines

26

Developing your freehand sketching

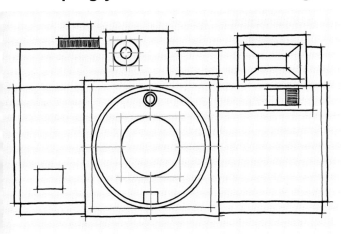

Fig. 2.18

So far, the practice exercises in this chapter have been designed to help you get used to holding a pencil correctly and to increase your confidence in using one. The suggestions for practice on these pages will help you to develop your skills further and enable you to sketch circles and curves by showing you how to construct simple frames or guidelines within which to draw. The camera in Fig. 2.18 has been drawn in this way. Remember to keep your pencil sharp, and aim to draw as freely and as quickly as possible. Avoid the temptation to use a ruler or straight edge – you must learn to control the pencil yourself.

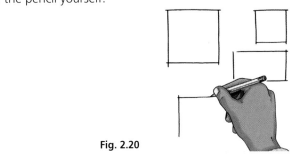

Fig. 2.20

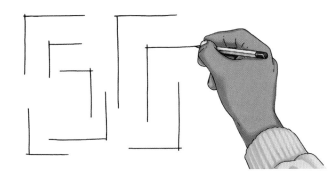

Fig. 2.19

1 Once you are confident drawing horizontal and vertical lines, try the exercise shown in Fig. 2.19. It consists of drawing right angles. Begin by drawing a vertical line and then draw a horizontal line at one of the ends of the vertical line, at right angles to it. Draw quickly and keep your hand moving, supported by your little finger if necessary.

2 After you have practised drawing right angles, try joining them together to form squares and rectangles (Fig. 2.20).

This is a very valuable exercise because most objects that you are likely to want to draw can be simplified and drawn as basic geometric shapes. Drawn lightly, these squares and rectangles can be used as frames for drawing other shapes. The next exercise (Fig. 2.21) shows how circles and ellipses can be constructed within a simple square or rectangular framework.

3 Circles and ellipses can be easily sketched freehand if you draw a simple frame to guide you. To draw a circle, begin by lightly drawing a freehand square the same width as the required diameter of the circle.

Find the approximate centre of each side and mark it with a short line, as shown in Fig. 2.21. This is the point where the circle will touch the square.

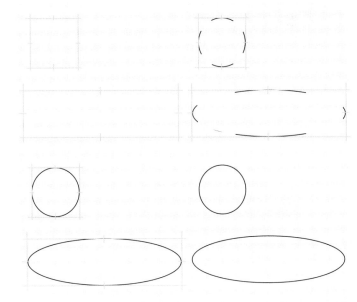

Fig. 2.21

An ellipse is constructed in a similar way, except that a rectangle, rather than a square, is drawn as the frame. Again, mark the points where the ellipse will touch the sides of the rectangle.

Begin drawing in the shape of the circle or ellipse by sketching a small arc at each point where the shape touches the frame. Gradually extend the arcs until they meet each other to form the outline shape. Sketch the shape very lightly, and then, when you are happy with it, make the outline stronger by pressing more firmly or going over it with a softer pencil.

3-DIMENSIONAL DRAWING

The drawing that you have done so far has been 2-dimensional (i.e. it has represented height and width to show one view or side of an object). In reality, most objects have not only an outline shape, they also have a solid form. So, when drawing objects to make them look realistic, you need to be able to represent their depth, as well as their height and width, to show all 3 dimensions.

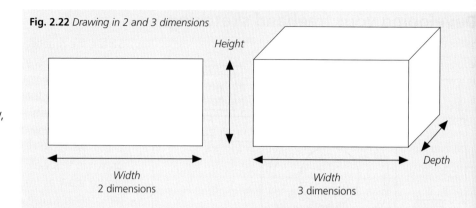

Fig. 2.22 *Drawing in 2 and 3 dimensions*

Height

Width
2 dimensions

Width
3 dimensions

Depth

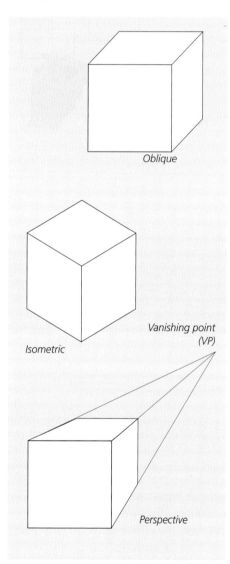

Oblique

Isometric

Vanishing point (VP)

Perspective

Fig. 2.23 *Types of 3 dimensional drawing*

There are several methods of creating 3-dimensional pictorial drawings. They can be drawn freehand or with the help of drawing instruments. At this stage try drawing freehand as it will help you to develop your sketching skills.

Oblique

This is the easiest method of 3-dimensional drawing. Draw the front view as normal and then add the top and sides by drawing lines at **45 degrees** from it. This is an **oblique** drawing.

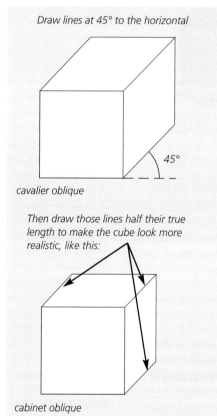

Draw lines at 45° to the horizontal

45°

cavalier oblique

Then draw those lines half their true length to make the cube look more realistic, like this:

cabinet oblique

Fig. 2.24 *Constructing an oblique drawing*

Oblique gives an accurate view of the front of the object, but when making measured oblique drawings you will find that the top and sides appear out of proportion if you draw them to their true length. To overcome this the **45 degrees** lines are drawn at half their true length (Fig. 2.24). This is known as **cabinet**

oblique and drawings with full length sides are known as **cavalier oblique**.

Isometric

In isometric drawings the horizontal lines of the object are drawn at an angle of **30 degrees**, (Fig. 2.25). Like the oblique drawing, it shows three sides but here they all appear slightly distorted. Drawing isometric views requires more practice than the oblique technique, but the results tend to look more realistic.

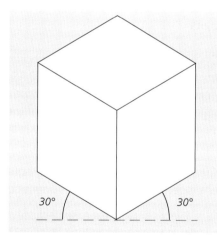

30°   30°

Fig. 2.25 *Isometric drawing*

Perspective

The most realistic 3-dimensional drawings are made using perspective-drawing techniques. There are several ways of making perspective drawings using a number of different 'vanishing points' (these are explained later in this chapter). For the time being, when sketching cubes, make all the horizontal lines converge at one vanishing point (**single-point perspective**) as shown in the perspective drawing in Fig. 2.23.

Planometric

This is another method of drawing which gives a 3-dimensional view. **Planometric drawings** are made from a simple plan view. The vertical lines are projected upwards at an angle of 45 degrees. The top of the finished drawing is the true shape of the object in the same way as the front of an oblique drawing is.

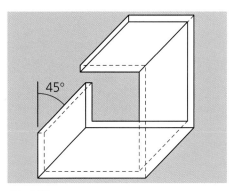

Fig. 2.26

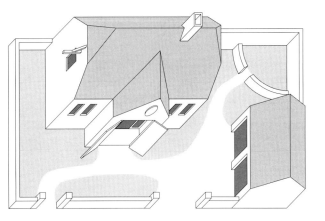

Planometric drawings are often used by architects to help people understand building plans. They are also useful in Graphic Products for showing displays and exhibition design.

Fig. 2.27 *An architectural planometric drawing*

Crating

So far, your drawing has mostly consisted of straight lines, boxes and cubes, which are important in helping you to construct more detailed drawings. Most objects are easier to draw if you begin by drawing them as simple, basic geometric shapes and forms, adding the detail later (Fig. 2.28).

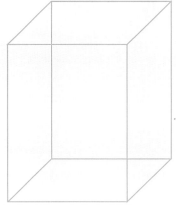

Construct the crate first – faintly

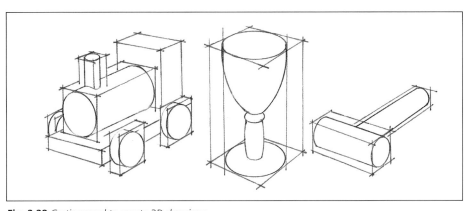

Fig. 2.28 *Crating used to create 3D drawings*

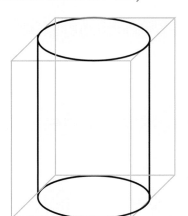

Sketch in the shape

The technique of drawing a box within which to construct your drawing is known as **'crating'**. Imagine an object fitted tightly into a box or crate. It is such a good fit that it does not rattle or move about – in fact it touches the crate at several points. Fig. 2.29 shows a cylinder which has been drawn by first constructing a crate and then sketching the cylinder within it. All curves, circles and ellipses can be drawn using this technique. First draw the crate, marking the points where the object will touch it, and then draw in the shape.

Any 3-dimensional drawing method can be used to draw crates – oblique, isometric or perspective.

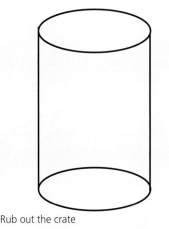

Rub out the crate

Useful tip

Construct your drawing with a 2H pencil and then draw in the outline and details with an HB.

Fig. 2.29 *Using crating to construct a cylinder*

Ken Allen (who is pictured on the left) has a wide experience in the construction industry, and his staff includes architects, building surveyors, senior and junior technicians, designers and chartered town planners. Together they form CAD Associates, architects and design consultants based in Lincoln.

The first stage of any project consists of the prospective client supplying an initial brief outlining the purpose of the building, size, site information, budget available, etc. From this, CAD Associates produce provisional line drawings. If the client is happy with these, a more detailed brief is written which enables CAD Associates to come up with design schemes in colour and in perspective to illustrate to their customers what the project will look like.

PERSPECTIVE DRAWING

The most realistic way of representing large 3-dimensional design ideas is through perspective drawing. Unlike the forms of 3-dimensional drawing described so far, perspective drawing gives the impression of depth and distance by taking into account the fact that horizontal lines appear to converge at some imaginary point in the distance.

You can see this by looking at buildings, straight roads or railway lines.

Fig. 2.30

We naturally see things in perspective, so drawings done in this way can appear very lifelike (Fig. 2.30)

Fig. 2.31

*CAD Associates have used **single-point perspective** to produce this drawing of the north elevation of the Hartpury College in Gloucestershire. As you can see, trees and other foreground details have been sketched in to give depth.*

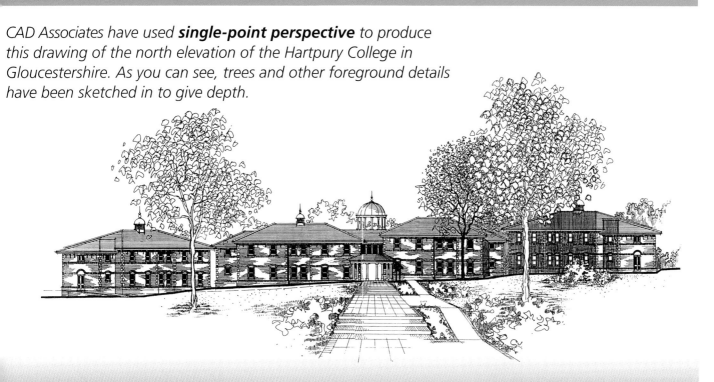

Single-point perspective

The single-point perspective technique shows objects 'flat on', rather like oblique drawing. Lines are taken from each corner to a single common vanishing point. The dice shown in Fig. 2.32 has been drawn using this method. The position of the vanishing point is important. If it is placed too close to the object the drawing will be too distorted.

Fig. 2.32

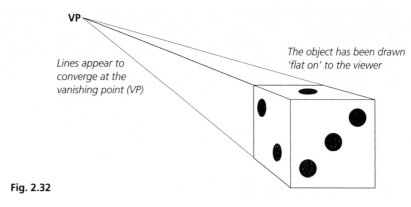

Lines appear to converge at the vanishing point (VP)

The object has been drawn 'flat on' to the viewer

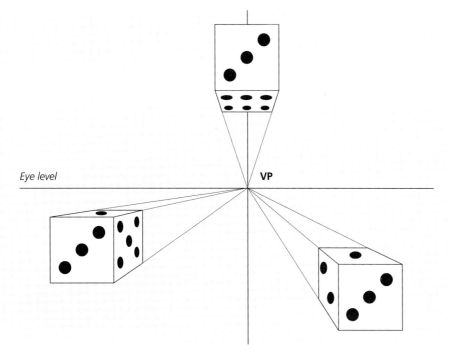

Eye level

VP

Viewpoints

A number of different viewpoints can be created with perspective drawing, depending upon where you position the vanishing point in relation to the object.

For instance, it is possible to create worm's eye views and bird's eye views of objects, and achieve some very dramatic effects by changing the position of the vanishing point.

When you are using single-point perspective drawing, decide which viewpoint will enable you to show the information or details that you wish to convey and then position the vanishing point accordingly.

Fig. 2.33 *Different effects can be achieved by moving the vanishing point in relation to the object*

31

*In the drawing of the office block shown on the left, CAD Associates have used **two-point perspective**. It has been used to illustrate a particular project in a promotional leaflet which is sent out to potential tenants and buyers. At the same time, working drawings, including a specification, are also prepared in order to apply for planning permission, and to be used in the actual construction.*

Two-point perspective

Two-point perspective enables you to draw objects at an angle to the viewer. The horizontal lines of the object converge at two different vanishing points positioned on the horizon or eye-level line.

The series of diagrams in Fig. 2.35 shows the stages involved in making two-point perspective drawings.

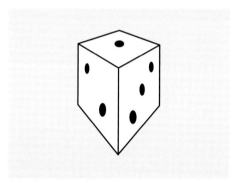

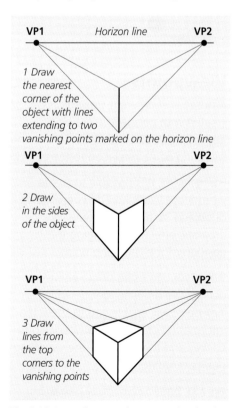

Fig. 2.35 *Stages in two-point perspective drawing*

Fig. 2.34 *A dice drawn in two-point perspective*

Multiple vanishing points

Sometimes, the shape or viewpoint of some objects that you want to draw may entail the use of three or four vanishing points.

The drawing of a skyscraper building in Fig. 2.36 has been drawn using three vanishing points.

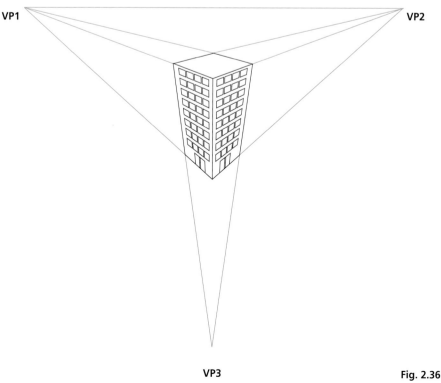

Fig. 2.36

32

The finished project, Doddington Court, can be seen in the photograph below.

*The publicity material for a local building project shown above illustrates the use of **multiple-vanishing-point perspective** in architectural drawing.*

The outline of the simple building in Fig. 2.37 uses four vanishing points.

In a complex drawing, such as the interior of a room, it is quite possible that you might need to use several different vanishing points to enable you to draw the room and its contents in the correct perspective.

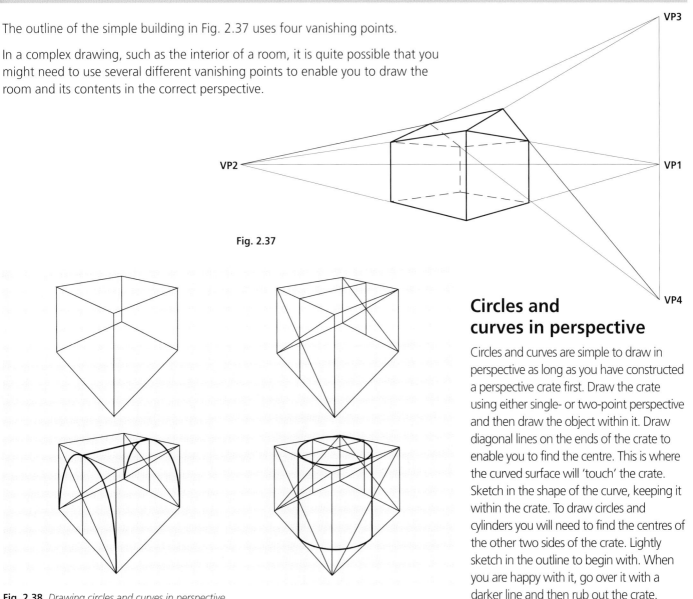

Fig. 2.37

Fig. 2.38 *Drawing circles and curves in perspective*

Circles and curves in perspective

Circles and curves are simple to draw in perspective as long as you have constructed a perspective crate first. Draw the crate using either single- or two-point perspective and then draw the object within it. Draw diagonal lines on the ends of the crate to enable you to find the centre. This is where the curved surface will 'touch' the crate. Sketch in the shape of the curve, keeping it within the crate. To draw circles and cylinders you will need to find the centres of the other two sides of the crate. Lightly sketch in the outline to begin with. When you are happy with it, go over it with a darker line and then rub out the crate.

33

SHAPE AND FORM

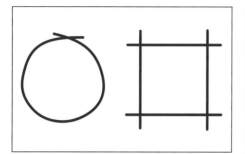

Fig. 2.39 *Lines are used to define space*

'Shape' is 2-dimensional – a flat area that is defined by lines. Random shapes can be created by drawing lines that cross over each other, as shown in Fig. 2.40. Shapes created in this way can be developed and used as decorative designs or pattern effects.

Fig. 2.40

Many of the objects around us consist of geometric shapes such as squares, rectangles, and triangles. This is true in nature too (natural honeycomb, for example, consists of 6-sided hexagonal shapes). In constructional terms, geometric shapes can be used to make very strong structures. It is important to consider this when working with sheet materials such as paper, card, metal, plastic and wood.

Fig. 2.41 *Geometric shapes are not just used in design drawings – they are all around us*

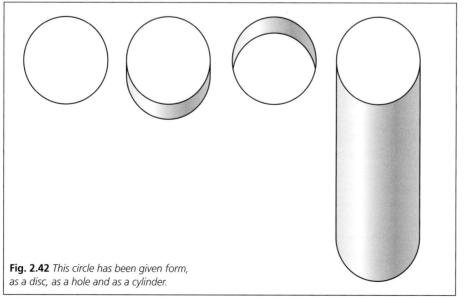

Fig. 2.42 *This circle has been given form, as a disc, as a hole and as a cylinder.*

Design ideas are often best communicated in 3 dimensions, using techniques such as oblique, isometric and perspective drawing (see Chapter 1). Three-dimensional drawing makes objects look solid and gives them 'form' as well as shape. When you portray form, you can give an impression of details such as size, proportion and weight. It is not possible to do this to the same extent using 2-dimensional drawing. Fig. 2.42 shows how a simple shape can be given form in order to create a number of 3-dimensional solid forms.

Light and shade

Drawing the effects of light and shade on objects can also be used to portray form. Simple shading with a pencil will give an indication of how light falls on the surfaces of an object. Think carefully about the imaginary position of the light source in your drawing, and remember that the areas of the object that are facing the light and those nearest to it will be lighter, while areas facing away from the light, or further away will be darker.

Shadows

Drawing the shadows from an object also helps portray its shape and form. Shadows can play an important part in design. For instance, architectural drawings sometimes show the estimated position of shadows because they may affect the visual appearance of the building.

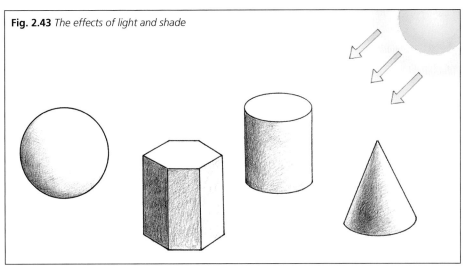

Fig. 2.43 *The effects of light and shade*

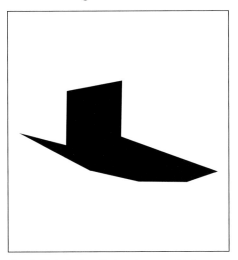

Fig. 2.44 *A shadow that portrays a cubic form*

When including shadows in a drawing it is important to remember that they also follow the rules of perspective. Shadows have their own vanishing point which is normally found where a line perpendicular from the light source (LS) intersects the horizon line. This point is usually marked 'VPS' or 'vanishing point of shadow'.

Fig. 2.45 *A shadow drawn in perspective*

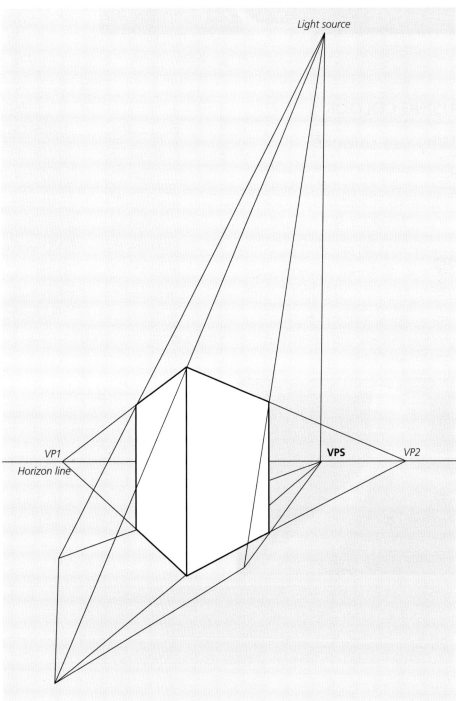

35

Colin Plant decided to pursue a career in graphic design after working in the printing department of an architects office. To achieve this, he went to college to obtain a National Diploma in graphic design and then studied at the University of Northumbria in Newcastle gaining a BA (Hons) in graphic design in 1996. Colin was employed by a design consultancy in London for five years and now works freelance.

The poster on the right is one of several that Colin produced for his diploma. It illustrates **colour harmony** *and was produced as an exercise in using gouache. The aim of the exercise was to create three distinct tones in all*

USING COLOUR

Why use colour?

Colour is used in the communication of design ideas for a number of reasons. It might simply be used to make a drawing look more attractive, or it might be used to highlight or draw attention to specific parts of a drawing (this is explained further on pp. 42–43). And like shading, colour can be used to portray the shape and form of an object. It also makes objects look more lifelike or realistic by giving an impression of the materials used to make them.

Fig. 2.46 *Here colour has beenused to highlight a chosen idea, and to show what material the object will be made of*

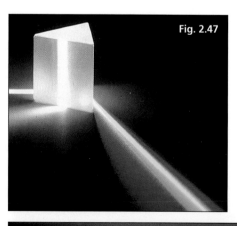

Fig. 2.47

Understanding colour

Using colour is not always as simple as you might first think. Applying too much colour or the wrong choice of colour will spoil a drawing. To use it to its best effect, you need to have an understanding of the theory of colour.

Natural light can be split into seven different colours (Fig. 2.47). These are called the colours of the spectrum.

They are red, orange, yellow, green, blue, indigo and violet. The colour of an object depends on how much of each of these colours is reflected or absorbed by it. For example, a red object reflects red light and absorbs the other colours. White objects reflect all colours, while black ones absorb all colours.

Colours have three elements, hue, chroma and tone. Hue describes a colour in general terms, for example red is the hue, while vermilion is the specific colour. Chroma describes the intensity or brightness of a colour and tone refers to the amount of black or white found in it.

Fig. 2.48 *The tonal range of a colour*

36

the colours used and to apply the colour flat and accurately. (Tones are created by adding white or black to colours, and are difficult to produce accurately.)

Typefaces that look interesting next to each other were chosen to give the image an eye-catching appearance.

Another of Colin's projects was to design a poster with a 1960s theme, which is shown on the next page. After researching typical posters of the period, he decided upon a hippy poster, as the hippy movement was a prominent and popular force of the era and is still well known today. Colin also wanted to include other important and celebrated symbols and icons such as John Lennon, the yin and yang signs and Che Guevara. He used bold colours of similar shades (oranges and reds) to reflect the psychedelia craze of the 1960s, and created the rounded, friendly-looking typeface for the same reason.

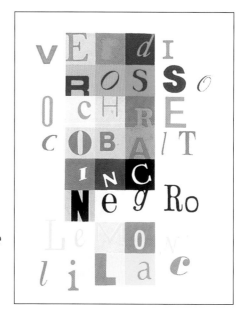

Primary colours

In design work, red, yellow and blue are known as the primary colours. This is because they are colours that cannot be created by mixing other colours together. All other colours can be made by mixing the primary colours together, in different proportions.

Fig. 2.49 The primary colours

Secondary colours

The three colours produced by mixing each of the primary colours together are known as secondary colours.

Fig. 2.50 The secondary colours

Tertiary colours

When a primary and a secondary colour are mixed together the result is known as a tertiary colour. Tertiary colours are subdued, earthy colours. They are useful for highlighting ideas because they allow the idea to stand out rather than the colour itself.

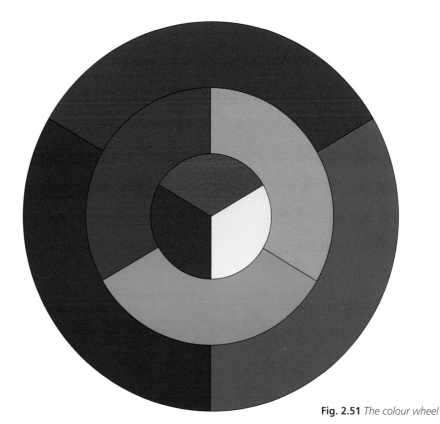

Fig. 2.51 The colour wheel

Over the years many complex models have been devised to show the relationships between the colours. A very simple way of understanding them is to imagine the three primary colours forming the centre of a wheel. In a ring around them are the colours produced by mixing them together, the secondary colours. In the outer ring is the range of

tertiary colours produced by mixing the primaries and secondaries together. The diagram in Fig. 2.51 shows this relationship very simply (e.g. red and yellow mix to produce orange), but it does not take into account the effect of tone (i.e. the results of adding black or white to a colour).

*The success and impact of this poster produced by Colin Plant are the result of the **colour interaction**, which creates discord and so grabs attention. The right-hand corner of the poster has been designed to look as if it has been torn off to reveal behind it an American poster protesting against the CIA and the Vietnam War. The lower part of the poster illustrates the use of colour harmony to create a soothing contrast.*

The brochure cover shown on the right was produced using only two colours – black and red. Fewer colours, used well, can often be more effective than using many. In this case, the theme of the brochure (vandalism) lends itself well to sparse use of stark, threatening colour. To give the image a dynamic impact and reflect the violent nature of vandalism, Colin juxtaposed the type and the logo and turned the design at an angle. After considering many typefaces, including handwritten and spray-can, he decided to use a computer-generated type because it had sharp edges and violent, ragged strokes.

THE EFFECTS OF COLOUR

Your designs, and people's understanding of your designs, can be greatly affected by the way you use colour. Some colours go well together, others don't. It is very important to remember this when using colours to help put across your ideas. The communication of good design ideas can be spoilt by a poor choice of colours.

To understand the relationship between colours and to see why they appear to react with each other we need to look at their position in the spectrum or on the colour wheel (Fig. 2.51, page 37).

Colour harmony

Colours that appear close to each other on the spectrum, such as orange and yellow, go well together and create harmony. It is important to consider this, for instance, when choosing colours for interior design. Rooms that are intended for peace and relaxation and that have to be lived in everyday need to have a harmonious colour scheme!

Fig. 2.53 *Colours in harmony*

Colour contrast

Colours from opposite ends of the spectrum can also be put together to good effect. Such colours are known as complementary colours and they create contrast. Complementary colours are used when you need to make things stand out vividly from other things around them. For instance, road signs need to contrast with the environment around them, so both shape and colour are used in their design to create visual tension.

Fig. 2.52 *Colour harmony has been used to good effect in this window display*

Fig. 2.54 *Colours creating contrast*

He used letratone to produce the grey colour – these are in fact black dots, but the eye sees it as grey. The photograph on the right shows a colour mock-up of the final design and the two colour- separated print masters. At this stage both masters are printed black. However, when the final print is made, they are put together and the bottom right section is printed in red.

Colin has also completed a number of various design projects for Cadbury's, Sainsbury's, Somerfield, Asda and the British Ecological Society.

Colour perception

The way we see colour and the effect that colour has on what we see always need to be considered when you are communicating your ideas. Some colours, for example, give us feelings of warmth or cold. Yellows, oranges and reds are warm colours while greens and blues are cold colours. If you look at coloured designs, you will see that warm colours appear to come towards you from the page, while cold colours go away from you. This impression of approaching and receding colours is useful when you need to highlight ideas on a page. Warm colours are more effective for this than cold colours.

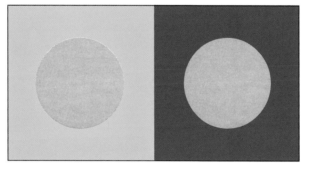

Fig. 2.56

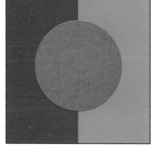

Fig. 2.57

Colours can have a similar effect on the way we perceive size and weight. Some colours, usually the warm range, can make objects look larger and heavier. This can be seen when two objects of the same size but different colours appear next to each other (Fig. 2.55).

The human eye always sees a colour in relation to at least one other colour. The way colours are seen and perceived is affected by background and adjacent colours. Look at the circles in the centre of the squares in Fig. 2.56. They are both exactly the same colour, but they appear to be different because our eyes see them in relation to the background.

The way you see the grey circle in Fig. 2.57 is affected by the colours either side of it. To prove this, lay your pencil vertically along the centre of the square. The circle will appear as two different shades of grey. This effect is known as 'simultaneous contrast' and is a good illustration of how the way we see colours is affected by other colours around us.

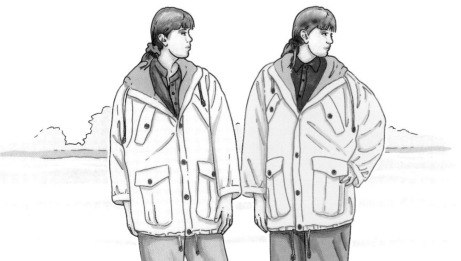

Fig. 2.55

39

DRY MEDIA

Coloured pencils

Coloured pencils are popular with professional illustrators and artists. They are very useful where subtle tones and colours are required, and for combining with other materials such as markers or paint. Water-soluble pencil crayons are also available. With these, when you have applied the colour to the paper, you can brush it with clean water to create watercolour effects.

Fig. 2.58 *A range of coloured pencils and an example of work using coloured pencils*

Pastels

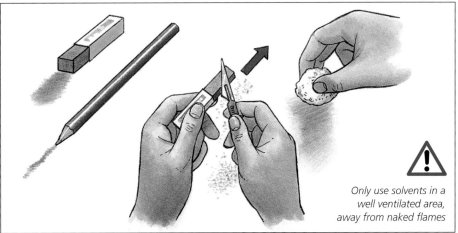

Only use solvents in a well ventilated area, away from naked flames

Fig. 2.59 *Using pastels for different effects and an example of pastel work*

Pastels are very versatile colouring materials. They are excellent for producing tonal effects and can create very effective and dramatic backgrounds on to which design ideas can be mounted. Pastels are available in either stick or pencil form. They can be applied directly on to paper, like chalk, or they can be painted on with cloth or cotton wool. To paint with pastels, you first need to scrape the pastel into a fine powder with a sharp knife. You then apply the powder to the paper with cloth or cotton wool that has been dipped into Clean Art fluid or a petroleum-based lighter fuel. (Take care when using flammable liquids and be sure NOT to use butane gas.) When used in this way the fluid evaporates and the powder is fixed to the paper, so it does not require a fixative spray. However, pastels that have been applied directly to the paper will need to be fixed to prevent them from smudging.

Markers

There are two types of coloured markers: water-based and spirit-based. Water-based markers are inexpensive and available in the form of felt-tipped pens, which are used for general colouring purposes. The ink is water soluble and takes a few seconds to dry, which can cause the paper to wrinkle when used to colour large areas. Felt-tipped pens are convenient and particularly useful when highlighting and colouring design ideas. Spirit-based markers are usually more expensive. They are mainly used for presentation work, often combined with coloured pencils or pastels. The use of markers is covered in more detail in 'Looking Good', the next chapter in this book.

Fig. 2.60 *Markers and an example of marker work*

40

WET MEDIA

When working with wet media such as watercolours, gouache or acrylics you must remember to stretch the paper before beginning work. This will prevent the paper wrinkling when the paint is applied. First of all, you need to thoroughly wet the paper with clean water, either in a sink or a tray. Then drain off the excess water and lay the paper on a clean drawing board. Now stick the paper down on to the board with gummed paper tape and allow it to dry before you use it.

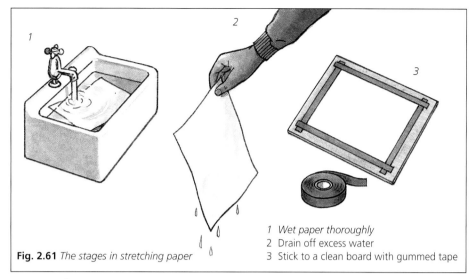

1 Wet paper thoroughly
2 Drain off excess water
3 Stick to a clean board with gummed tape

Fig. 2.61 *The stages in stretching paper*

Watercolour

Fig. 2.62

In design work, watercolour is used mainly as a wash to highlight areas of drawings to draw attention to them, or to create tones to portray form. It is applied as a thin transparent wash, which tints the drawing. Denser areas of colour are built up by applying more layers of the wash. Fig. 2.62 shows how a series of colour washes can be applied to create a light and shade effect on a cube.

Watercolours are available in two different grades: artists' colours, which are made from high-quality pigments and are very expensive; and students' colours which are more reasonably priced and perfectly adequate for the design and technology work that you will be doing.

Gouache

Gouache is an opaque form of watercolour similar to poster paint. It is very useful when strong, dense colour is required, and is very good for painting card models. Gouache is available in jars or tubes (Fig. 2.63) and is water soluble, so your brushes can be easily cleaned in water even after the paint has dried on them.

Fig. 2.63

Acrylics

Watercolours and gouache have been used as painting materials for several hundred years. More recently, acrylics have also become available. They were developed in the 1930s to provide a paint that was tough enough to be used for murals in very exposed positions. To achieve this resilience the colour pigment is bound in a synthetic resin, which is made from a plastic material called polyvinyl acetate (PVA).

Acrylic paint is very versatile. It can be applied as a thin wash like watercolour or as dense, opaque colour like gouache.

It is important to remember that acrylic paint is quick-drying, so the screw tops on the tubes must be kept clean and replaced. And because it is plastic based, it is very difficult to remove from brushes if it is allowed to dry.

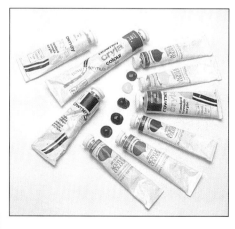

Fig. 2.64 *Tubes of acrylic and a novel design for a barcode, painted using acrylics*

41

HIGHLIGHTING IDEAS

In the early stages of designing, your graphic work will often consist of sheets of initial ideas, quickly sketched as you have thought of them. The next stage is to highlight the ideas that you want to refine and develop further. Highlighting draws the viewer's attention to ideas. It can also be used to separate good ideas from unsuitable ones. Highlighting can be carried out in a number of different ways using line, tone and colour.

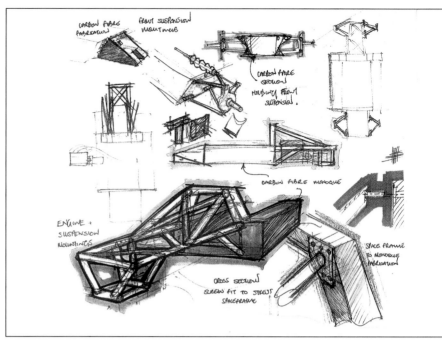

Fig. 2.65 *Highlight ideas that you want to develop further*

Weighted line

One way of highlighting ideas is by using what is known as a 'weighted line'. This involves drawing a darker or thicker line around the outline of the drawing you want to highlight. A weighted line has the effect of lifting the selected drawing away from those around it on the page. This technique can be used on both pencil and ink drawings. When working in pencil, you need to use a softer grade to make a darker line. When working in ink, use a wider nib or pen tip. Fig. 2.66 shows how a weighted line can be used.

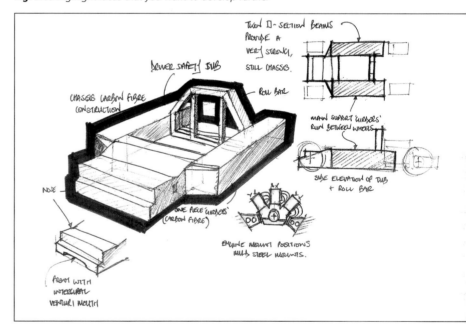

Fig. 2.66

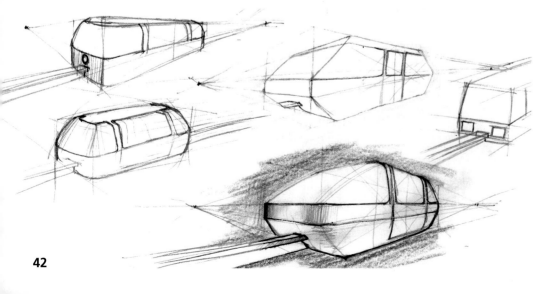

Tone

To highlight an idea using tone, shade an area around the outline of your chosen drawing (a pencil is usually used for this). Graduated tone can be effectively created by gradually increasing the pressure of the pencil on the paper.

Fig. 2.67 *An idea highlighted using tone*

Colour

Almost any coloured media can be used to highlight design ideas. There are special pens available for highlighting text, but they are not always suitable for using on drawings because their ink is too bright. This can give an overpowering effect, with the highlighter colour standing out vividly and the idea becoming lost in the glare. The rule for using highlighter pens is to use them with care – try them out on a piece of scrap paper first.

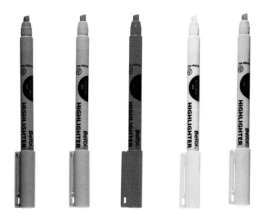

Fig. 2.68 *Highlighter colour can be useful. Here it has been used to good effect to draw attention to part of a drawing. Be careful when using highlighter pens – do not let the colour overpower your drawings.*

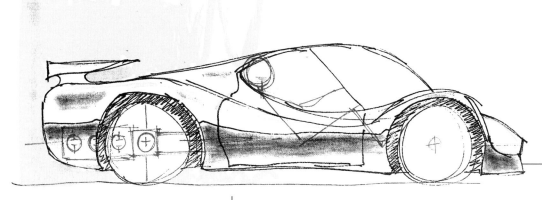

REAR ENGINED, REAR WHEEL DRIVE.

When you are highlighting an idea, choose the colour carefully. You will often find that the more subdued, subtle colours are more effective than bright ones. Marker pens, pastels, gouache, watercolour and acrylics are all suitable. The most common technique is to apply the colour around the selected idea to make it stand out (Fig. 2.69).

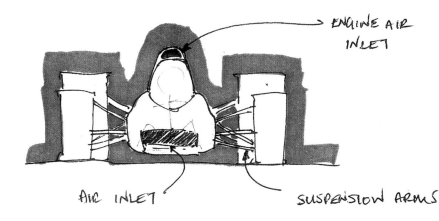

ENGINE AIR INLET

AIR INLET

SUSPENSION ARMS

Fig. 2.69

Colour can also be applied directly over an idea to highlight details such as how it is assembled or to show how it works. In this case the colour needs to be thin enough for the details of the drawing to show through. You will also need to apply colour directly to the drawing when some indication of the finished colour or the materials to be used is required.

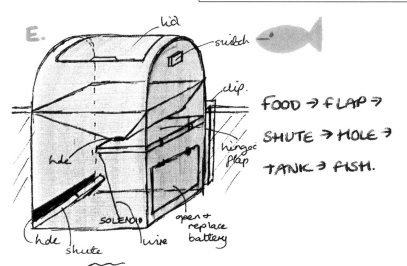

Fig. 2.70 *Colour has been applied directly over this drawing of a fish feeder to emphasise its details*

43

BARKING DOG ART
design & illustration

Barking Dog Art is a graphic design company which was established 14 years ago, primarily producing artwork for academic publishers. Back then the work was carried out using Rotring pens, stencil sets, french curves, rub-down letraset text and patterns, and tracing paper on a drawing board.

10 years ago Mike Parsons, Graphic Designer/Illustrator, invested in an Apple Macintosh computer, Adobe Illustrator illustration software, and a black and white printer and scanner Black and white diagrams were produced on the computer, printed and then used as final artwork by academic publishers. For the publishers themselves, this was too advanced for them to do in-house. Now, approximately 95% of Barking Dog Art's work is generated using a computer. In fact the drawing board is of no use any longer in the studio.

WORKING WITH INK

Ink is a very versatile medium for communicating design ideas. It can be used at all stages of design, from sketching initial ideas to technical drawing (using a technical pen). And if you use a brush to apply it, ink can be used for highlighting ideas or painting in areas of colour.

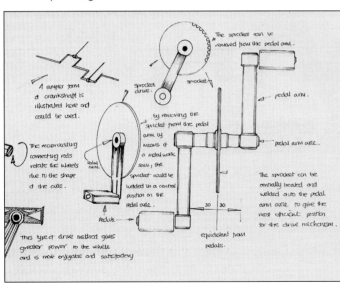

Fig. 2.71 *Ink has many uses in communicating design – from technical drawing to highlighting ideas*

Fig. 2.72 *Inks and pens:*
a) dip pen;
b) felt-tip pen;
c) technical pen

Inks

You can buy ink in a variety of colours as well as traditional black drawing ink. Some ink manufacturers produce between 15 and 20 different colours. There are also different types of ink available. For example, artists' drawing ink is waterproof and dries as a glossy film; non-waterproof inks dry to a matt finish and can be diluted with distilled water if required.

Pens

There is a wide range of pens available for drawing, from simple dip pens to the highly specialist technical pens used for technical drawing and draughting. Dip pens do not have a built-in ink reservoir, so need to be dipped directly into the ink. You can buy a large number of nibs for them to enable you to produce a variety of line widths.

Felt- and fibre-tipped pens are made with both waterproof and water-soluble inks and in a variety of thicknesses. They are a clean and convenient way of using ink.

For accurate drawing, technical pens are available in a number of line widths ranging from 0.1 mm to 2.0 mm. The ink flows through a delicate hollow nib which must be treated with great care. Special inks are used in technical pens – normal waterproof ink would dry and clog the nib.

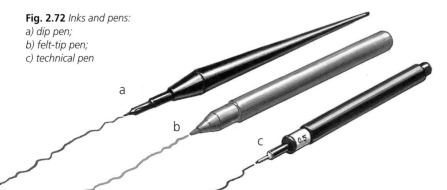

The name Barking Dog Art was influenced by Mike's family German Shepherd, Coni. Mike did not want the name to be too serious such as 'Parson's Design Associates'. Also by using the word 'Art' as opposed to 'Illustration', the business activities can diversify into different areas such as graphics, web design, and logo design, etc.

Barking Dog Art continues to work heavily in the publishing business, producing book layouts and illustrations for primary, A-Level and academic products. The work carried out now involves using new technological software such as interactive CD-ROMs and the internet in producing these illustrations.

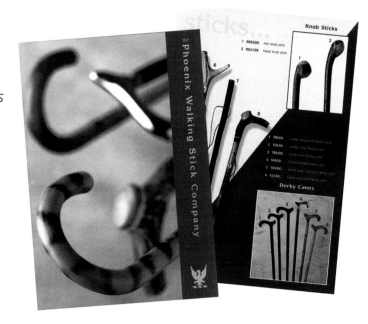

Using a brush

You can use a brush to apply ink, either 'neat' – straight from the bottle – or diluted with water to make a wash. Different tones can be produced by adding layers of an ink wash, just as you would when working with watercolour.

Good quality brushes should be used. Traditionally, brushes were made of sable. You can still buy sable brushes today, but they are expensive, and satisfactory results can be achieved with the cheaper modern nylon brushes. Whatever brush you do use, it should be cleaned thoroughly after use (waterproof ink is very difficult to remove once it has dried).

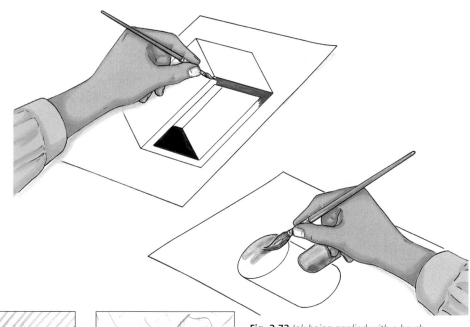

Fig. 2.73 *Ink being applied with a brush*

Ink effects

You can create a huge variety of effects when working with ink. You don't have to limit yourself to applying ink with a pen or a brush – you can use almost anything. Try making your own dip pen from a sharpened stick (take care if you use a sharp blade). You could even dab ink on with a sponge, or spatter it on using your old toothbrush!

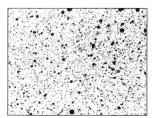

1 Lines *2 Cross hatching* *3 Scribbles*

4 Dots *5 Spatter from a toothbrush* *6 Ink wash*

Fig. 2.74 *Examples of effects possible with ink*

Barking Dog Art also offers creative graphic design for other commercial businesses. They produce designs for brochures, catalogues, marketing material, corporate identities, signage and web-sites. Their clientele includes Reading and Bristol University,

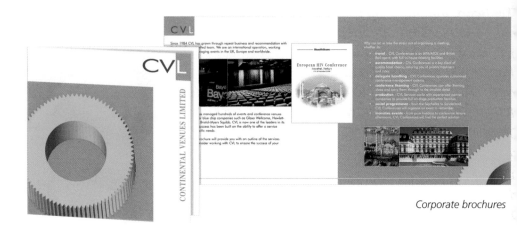

Corporate brochures

Cheltenham Ladies College, Westbury Homes, as well as HarperCollins Publishers. Barking Dog Art also look after complementing design services such as reprographics, print and photography.

RENDERING

To make your design drawings look more realistic you can give them texture by using simple graphic techniques. This is known as 'rendering'. You can use a variety of media to achieve realistic effects and to show the materials that are to be used to make your designs. Ink, graphite and coloured pencils, pastels, paint and markers can be used either on their own or in various combinations. Some computer-graphics software packages have rendering facilities that enable products to be visualised on screen before printing out on to paper.

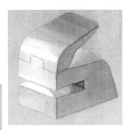

Fig. 2.75 *This design for a hole punch has been rendered to make it look more realistic*

Wood

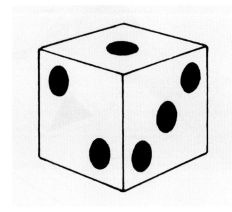

Fig. 2.76

Fig. 2.76 shows a design drawing for a dice, but it is not possible to tell what it is to be made from. Simple rendering will enable you to show the materials that are to be used to construct what you have designed.

a

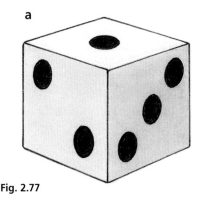

b

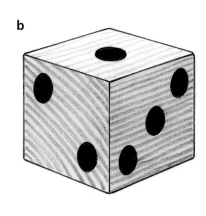

Fig. 2.77

Let us suppose that the dice is to be made of wood. You can use coloured pencils very effectively to give an impression of wood grain.

Begin rendering by shading in a background colour. This should be a pale yellow or a light brown depending on the type of wood to be used. Don't forget to show the effect of light and shade by making the surface facing the light source the lightest, as shown in Fig. 2.77a. Next, using a darker shade, draw in the grain of the wood. This need not be too accurate but sufficient to give an impression of grain. It is a good idea to show the end grain on one of the surfaces, as shown in Fig. 2.77b.

The team at Barking Dog Art is made up of 3 full-time designers, including Mike, but also has a database of freelance workers who help out from time to time. This results in minimal overheads and flexibility in the quantity of work. For Barking Dog it is also important to keep their charges competitive without damaging the quality of work. Sometimes small companies such as Barking Dog Art find it difficult to prove to larger clients that because the company is small this does not necessarily mean that they cannot handle the volume of work or that they may be less effective. However, larger studios in design and marketing often incur larger overheads and larger fees.

Illustration example

Opaque plastic

Plastic materials can be rendered using coloured pencils or markers. If you need to render a polished or reflective surface you will have to consider reflections when you show light falling on the object. Light will be reflected off the edges and corners and is rendered as highlights (these are not to be confused with highlighting ideas to make them stand out). One way to represent highlights is to leave the areas where light is reflected white and let the paper show through. Alternatively, highlights can be put in with white coloured pencil, gouache or correcting fluid.

Lines to represent reflections can be drawn on the surfaces of the material using a white coloured pencil (Fig. 2.78b).

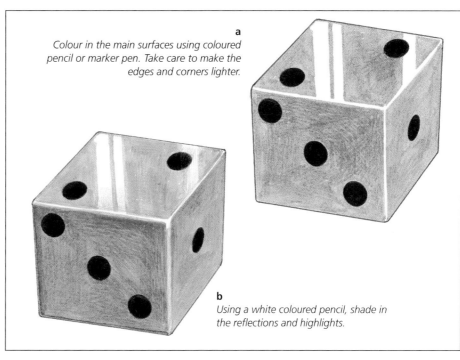

a
Colour in the main surfaces using coloured pencil or marker pen. Take care to make the edges and corners lighter.

b
Using a white coloured pencil, shade in the reflections and highlights.

Fig. 2.78 *Rendering opaque plastic to show highlights and reflections*

Transparent plastic and glass

Transparent materials such as plastic and glass are a little more difficult to render because they have no natural colour of their own. An effective method is to use blue or green pencils to shade the surfaces, and leave areas of white paper to represent the reflections. The cube in Fig. 2.79 was rendered by shading each of the six surfaces separately.

The transparent effect can be increased if you include a background in your drawing. Drawing in a background first and then rendering the object in front of it will ensure that it appears to be transparent.

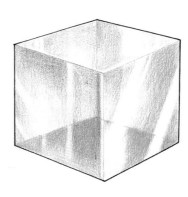

Fig. 2.79 *Rendering transparent objects*

Metal and polished surfaces

Metals with a dull or matt surface are very easy to render. First of all, you need to give an impression of the overall colour, and then show the effect of the light falling on it by varying the tones and adding highlights, as shown in Fig. 2.80. As with rendering other materials, reflections can be added with a white coloured pencil, but do remember that on a matt surface they will blend into the main colour and not contrast as much as reflections on a shiny surface.

Fig. 2.80

Fig. 2.81

Highly polished surfaces and metals such as polished silver, chrome and brass do not show much of their own colour. They are rather like mirrors in that they reflect the objects around. This can make them difficult to render. Illustrators and graphic artists have overcome this problem by adopting a technique of rendering known as the 'desert landscape'. This technique involves representing the sky and the desert as if they are reflected on to the polished surface. The upper surfaces of the object reflect the sky and the lower part the ground. Fig. 2.81 shows a cylinder and a sphere rendered in this way.

Step 1	Step 2	Step 3
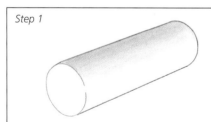		
Begin by colouring in the top part of the drawing as the sky. Coloured pencils or pastels are the best media for producing a graduated effect.	Next, working down from the horizon, fill in the ground area. Graduate the colour – start with a dark shade at the top, getting lighter towards the bottom.	Finally, add a graduated sky effect to the end of the object and put in highlights around the edge.

Fig. 2.82 *Steps in rendering a polished surface*

The dice in Fig. 2.83 gives the impression of being polished. This effect has been created by showing the background reflected in it, which convinces our eye that it must be a highly polished, reflective surface. The top surface has a graduated blue tint to reflect the imaginary sky.

Fig. 2.83

48

Textures

The texture of a material can be effectively rendered in a variety of ways. Texture effects are particularly useful when rendering objects which have a 'rough' surface, like the ones shown in Fig. 2.84.

Texture created using ink

Dry transfer texture

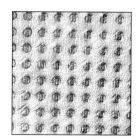

Texture created using a texture pad

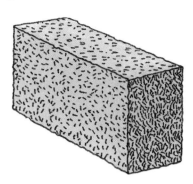

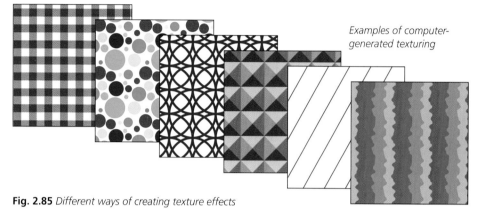

Examples of computer-generated texturing

Fig. 2.85 *Different ways of creating texture effects*

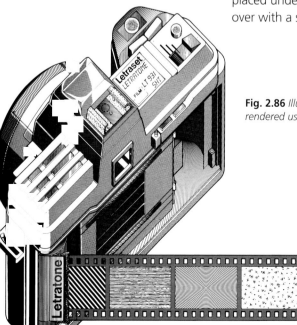

Fig. 2.84 *Textures created to show the rough surfaces of concrete and leather*

Fig. 2.85 illustrates some of the methods you can use to create textured effects. You can use ink in a variety of ways (Fig. 2.74). There is also a large range of dry transfer textures available, which can be applied by rubbing the transfer on to the drawing in the same way as instant lettering. Often, computer-graphics software has a good range of textures which are useful for rendering. Alternatively, a textured surface can be placed under the paper and then shaded over with a soft pencil.

Texture pads can be bought in a wide range of textures, but there are many objects and materials available around your house or the classroom that will work just as well. For instance, the plastic cases from old radios and tape recorders often have an imitation leather surface. Perforated metal and old speaker grills can create an effective textured look. If you are rendering a fabric surface, try a sheet of coarse glass paper under your drawing.

Place your paper over your 'texture' and rub with a soft pencil, just as if you were making a coin or brass rubbing. Try it – you will find the results are very effective.

Fig. 2.86 *Illustration of a camera rendered using dry transfer textures*

Fig. 2.87 *A pupil using a textured surface for rendering*

MARKERS

Spirit-based markers (also known as 'permanent' markers) are very suitable for presentation work because they have a wide range of colours and tones that dry quickly without wrinkling the paper.

Some brands of markers can be matched exactly with printing inks, paper and card colours. This enables designers to show the precise colour they propose to use.

If you do colour your drawings with permanent markers, you will need to use special 'bleed-proof' paper to prevent the ink from spreading (bleeding) over the outlines before it dries. The ink may also bleed through to the other side of the paper. Designers sometimes take advantage of this when they want to produce a pale or subdued colour. They turn the paper over and apply the marker on the reverse, allowing it to bleed through to the other side and create the effect they want.

Fig 2.88 *Cutaway of a marker pen, showing the padding and ink inside and a close up of a chisel point and a pointed point.*

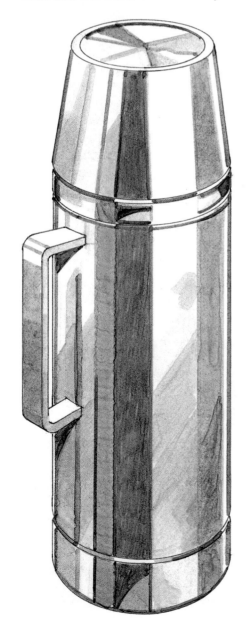

Markers can be used on their own to present your design ideas, or they can be used in conjunction with other graphic media such as pastels or coloured pencils.

Figure 2.89 shows examples of drawings of metal and plastic objects that have been rendered using marker pens. The marker has been used to give form to the objects and to give an indication of the material they are made from. This has been achieved by using light, shade, reflections and highlights.

Fig 2.89 *These objects have been rendered with markers to show that they are made from metal and plastic*

The personal CD player shown in Figure 2.90 has been rendered using a combination of markers and coloured pencils. The coloured pencils have been used to produced graduated tones on the body of the CD player and to show reflections on its surface. The highlights have been painted in with 'process white', which is a form of poster paint used by graphic designers. The fine details have been added using a technical pen (fine-line marker pens can also be used to add these finishing touches to your drawings). The finished result is a very effective drawing with an almost photographic quality. Drawings rendered in this way are often used as illustrations for brochures and advertisements – they are also an excellent way of showing people what you think your finished design will look like.

Fig 2.90 *The high-quality rendering of this personal CD player gives it an almost photographic appearance.*

Basic marker techniques

Many people using markers for the first time tend to use them to colour the work rather like using a crayon. The resulting work can appear messy and less than satisfactory. With some basic marker techniques and a little practice some very effective results can be obtained in a short time.

Marker pens are available with two types of tips, a pointed or bullet shaped tip and a chisel tip. The pointed tips are used for drawing and outlining while the chisel tip is used for laying down areas of solid colour and filling in large areas. Chisel tips however, can also be used on their edge to produce thin lines. Some marker manufacturers produce pens with both types of tips, one in each end.

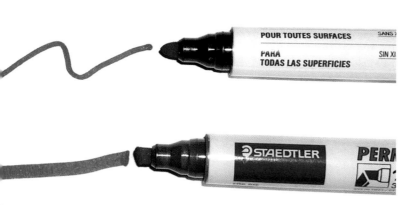

Fig 2.91 Marker pen tips

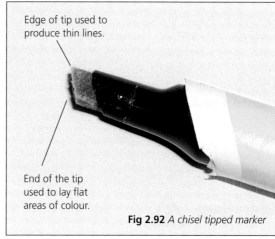

Edge of tip used to produce thin lines.

End of the tip used to lay flat areas of colour.

Fig 2.92 A chisel tipped marker

Laying flat areas of colour

Flat areas of colour can be laid using a chisel tipped marker. Large, even areas of colour can be produced by moving the tip horizontally across the paper allowing each strip of colour to butt up to the previous one without overlapping. You will need to work quickly taking care not to allow the tip to stop on the page and create a blot of darker colour.

Fig 2.93 Laying an area of colour

Producing different tones

Different tones of the same colour can be obtained by going over the area with the marker several times. Darker tones are produced in this way can be used to show light and shade and give form to an object as shown in fig 2.94.

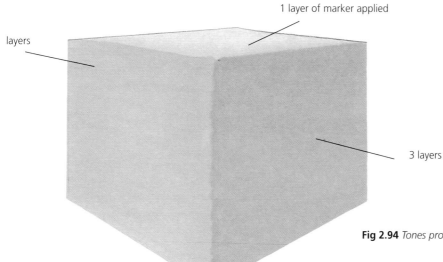

1 layer of marker applied

layers

3 layers

Fig 2.94 Tones produced with 3 layers of marker.

Masking

It is difficult to achieve crisp lines around marker work, even when using bleedproof paper. Many graphic designers cut out their work and mount it on a new background. It is also possible to mask out an area to be coloured with either masking tape or masking film used for airbrushing. (See page 55). Always test the paper first to make sure that the tape will not tear the surface of the paper. Masking will not give a perfect edge because the ink will bleed under the tape but it is much better than working up to a line.

Fig 2.95 *Using masking tape*

Blending

Blending marker work with lighter fuel or clean art fluid allows you to produce an even layer of colour. It can also be used to produce an area of colour which graduates from light to dark. The fluid is applied with a cotton bud or a piece of cotton wool. Take care to use it in a well ventilated place, away from naked flames.

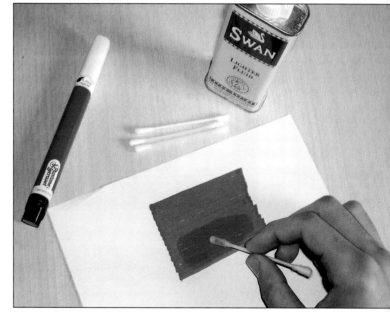

Fig 2.96 *Blending using lighter fuel*

Fig 2.97 *Before blending*

Fig 2.98 *After blending*

Spraying

Marker ink can be sprayed on to paper using the LetraJet Air Marker System. When connected to a compressor or a can of compressed air ink is blown from the marker pen on to the artwork. Graduated backgrounds and tonal effects can be produced as well as a whole range of airbrush effects. (See pages 54 & 55.) Markers can be used again for drawing by simply unclipping from the air marker unit.

Fig 2.99 *The LetraJe Air Marker Syster*

Safety note – Take care when using compressed air and never point it at your skin. Do not puncture compressed air cans.

Using markers – step by step

The illustrations on this page show you, step-by-step, how to make presentation drawings using markers and coloured pencils.

First of all, you need to make an accurate drawing. The drawing in Figure 2.100 has been made using two-point perspective. You can use any method of pictorial drawing, but perspective drawing will enable you to choose the most suitable viewpoint and to produce a realistic effect. Figure 2.100 was drawn using a 2H pencil.

In Figure 2.101, the first layer of colour has been carefully applied with a marker. When you do this it is important to use the marker quickly and to try not to overlap or leave gaps between the strokes. To begin with, you may find it helpful to hold the tip of the marker against a straight edge (be careful not to smudge the colour when you move the edge). With a little practice you will be able to apply an even layer of colour in this way. Try it out yourself first on a piece of scrap paper.

Once you have blocked in the main colour, use a marker in a darker shade to create a tonal effect, similar to that shown in Figure 2.102, where darker areas have been added to help portray the form of the object. It is important at this stage that you decide where the light source will be so that you can add the tones according to its position. At this point, you can leave the main highlights as areas of clean white paper.

Figure 2.103 shows the finished drawing. Reflections have been added using a white coloured pencil, and graduated tones have been incorporated by applying coloured pencils in colours that correspond to the colours of the marker ink. All that remains is to add final details with a fine-line pen and small highlights with paint.

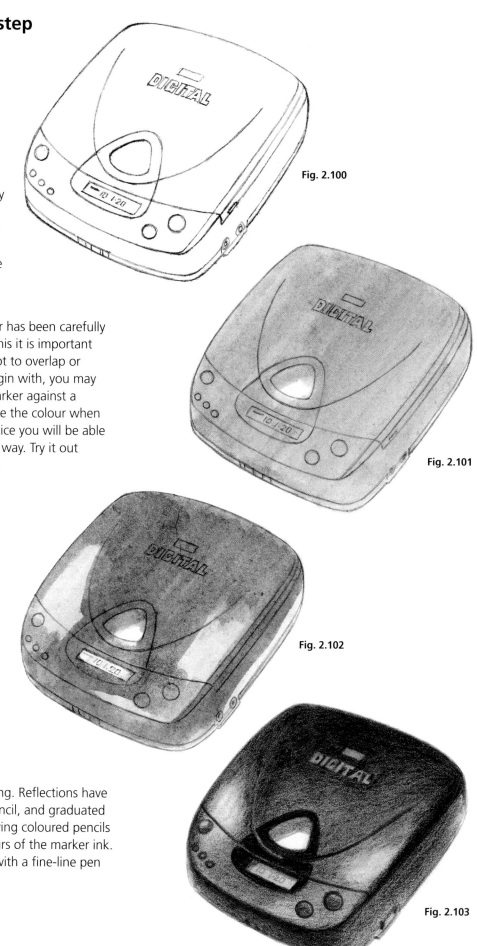

Fig. 2.100

Fig. 2.101

Fig. 2.102

Fig. 2.103

AIRBRUSHING

Airbrushes

Airbrushes are small spray guns that use a jet of air to spray a variety of liquid media on to paper. They can be used for colouring presentation drawings, rendering, and for painting models, and they can create very realistic effects of near-photographic quality.

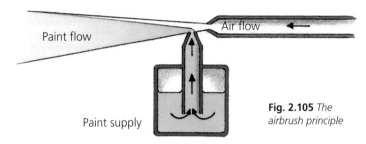

Paint flow

Air flow

Paint supply

Fig. 2.105 *The airbrush principle*

Fig. 2.104 *A double-action airbrush in use*

The airbrush was invented at the end of the nineteenth century. It was first used by a doctor to spray medicine into his patients' throats. The design has changed very little over the years – it is a delicately-engineered tool that has a needle with a matching nozzle to control the delivery of paint. The nozzle must be treated with care, and the airbrush must always be kept clean and well maintained if it is to give good results.

There are several types of airbrushes available, ranging from simple, single-action brushes to more sophisticated double-action types. The single-action mechanism gives you control over the air supply to the brush and is best suited to painting backgrounds and colouring models. For more detailed and complex work, you will need to use double-action airbrushes that allow control over the paint supply as well as the air supply.

The air supply

Airbrushes need compressed air in order to work. The most economical way of providing the necessary supply of air is to use a compressor. This is an electrically-operated pump which uses either a flexible diaphragm or piston to force the air through. You can also use aerosol cans of propellant, but they only allow a limited working time before the can needs replacing and they are only useful for small-scale work or when an airbrush is only occasionally used. In order to produce good-quality work, the supply of air must be clean and should not fluctuate. Moisture in the air can also cause problems – some more expensive compressors are fitted with filters and moisture traps to clean and dry the air.

Airbrush media

Almost any liquid can be applied with an airbrush, from liquid inks and dyes to suspended pigments such as oil paint and pottery glazes. You can also buy special paints for airbrushing in a wide range of colours. These are specially formulated for easy, clog-free use. Whatever liquid you do use, do not allow it to dry in the airbrush (particularly media such as Indian ink, acrylic and oil paints). Do make sure your airbrush is thoroughly cleaned out every time you use it and washed with an appropriate solvent. The solvent should be put in the reservoir and sprayed until the liquid coming through the nozzle of the airbrush is clear.

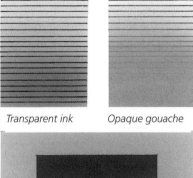

Transparent ink   *Opaque gouache*

Fig. 2.106 *Cans of aerosol propellant and a compressor*

Rectangle of gouache overlaid with transparent ink

⚠️ *Never blow compressed air onto anyone's skin and do not inhale spray paints; always wear a facemask.*

Fig 2.107 *Examples of different airbrushed media*

Masking

When you use an airbrush to colour your work, you need to plan ahead carefully. With any spray technique, there is a danger of unwanted overspray. To prevent this you need to make masks to cover the areas that you do not want to be sprayed. Simple masks can be made from scrap paper or newspaper, but for more complex work, masking film or masking fluid is more accurate and appropriate. Masking film is a low-tack plastic film rather like the clear film used to cover books and posters. It is stuck over the drawing, and the parts that require colouring are cut out with a scalpel and removed. After spraying, the cut-out piece of film is replaced and other areas are removed. Fig. 2.108 shows film being cut to mask an area of an airbrushed drawing. Masking fluid is a rubber-based material in an ammonia solution.

Fig. 2.108

It is painted on to the paper with a brush. The ammonia evaporates leaving behind a layer of rubber which acts as a resistant on the paper. After spraying, when the surface is dry, the rubber can be removed by gently rubbing with your finger.

Airbrush techniques

Airbrushes can be used to create a variety of different effects – from thin lines, produced by spraying up to a mask or a ruler, to solid areas of colour or graduated washes. When learning to use an airbrush for the first time, it is a good idea to practise the different techniques before attempting to airbrush a drawing (Fig. 2.109). Fig. 2.110 shows you the steps towards creating a good airbrushed drawing.

Fig. 2.109 *Airbrush techniques – lines, solid colour and graduated washes*

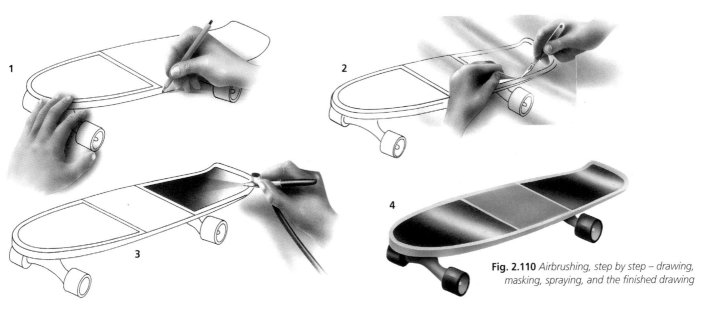

Fig. 2.110 *Airbrushing, step by step – drawing, masking, spraying, and the finished drawing*

PHOTOGRAPHY

Photography is a very useful medium in Graphic Products and can be used in most stages of the design process. You may want to take photographs as part of your investigation to help you identify opportunities for designing, keep a record of the development of your product or to record the testing of your finished work. Photography might be required in order to make the prototype of your product. Many graphic products would not exist without the use of photography in one form or another. Packaging and many examples of graphic design use images which were originally captured using photography. Modern ICT equipment allows you to make use of photography and image manipulation in your project work in a very similar way to that used in industry.

Fig. 2.111 *Examples of photography in graphic products*

Cameras and film

There are many different types of camera available, ranging from disposable ones to sophisticated professional equipment costing thousands of pounds.

Fig. 2.112

35 mm cameras

The most common type of camera is the 35 mm which is available in many different versions from simple point and shoot types to single lens reflex cameras which allow you to see exactly what you are taking in the viewfinder. Most modern cameras are perfectly adequate for your work in school but it is usually true that the better the camera, the better the results.

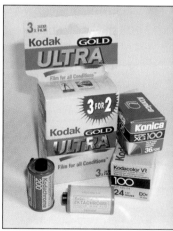

Fig. 2.113

35 mm cameras have a large range of films available to them. Films are sold with different speeds. This may sound complicated but it refers to how sensitive the film is to light. A slow film will not be very sensitive to light but will give very good quality pictures when exposed in the correct light. A fast film will take photographs in poor light conditions but will not produce as good quality photographs as a slow film. As a general rule, films with a speed of between 100 and 200 ASA (21 to 24 DIN) will provide good results in most conditions but you may need to use a flash when taking photographs indoors.

Instant cameras

There are two types of instant camera available which allow you to see your photographs within a few minutes of taking them. The quality of the photographs from instant cameras is not usually as good as 35 mm and the films are more expensive.

Digital cameras

There has been rapid development in digital camera technology. Inexpensive digital cameras are available for use in schools. The image is captured on a light sensitive device known as a **CCD (close coupled device)** which works in a similar way to a computer scanner. The picture is converted to digital data which allows it to be saved, usually as a JPEG file.

Fig. 2.114

56

Video cameras

Video is another form of instant photography. It is an excellent medium for recording your investigation and understanding how things work because you can play back in slow motion and freeze frame, allowing you to see exactly what is happening. Modern digital video cameras have a still facility which allows you to use them as a digital camera to take still photographs.

Fig. 2.115 *A digital video camera*

Using your photographs

It is possible to use photographs in your Graphic Products projects to produce brochures, booklets and packaging quite simply and without needing to use a darkroom. Computer technology allows us to manipulate images and use them in our design work in much the same way as it is done in industry. Before we can begin we need to get the images into the computer. This is simple if you have a digital camera. The photograph is either downloaded into the machine using the cameras software, transferred using a memory card or, in the case of some Sony cameras, directly by floppy disk or CD-ROM. Don't worry if you have not got access to a digital camera because many photographic developing companies will develop your photographs and convert them to digital images and save them onto a CD-ROM.

Fig. 2.116 *It is possible to create montages of images for your projects like this advertising photograph*

Scanning images

Photographs and artwork can be scanned into the computer using a flatbed scanner. The image is placed face down on the glass screen and the image is scanned like a photocopier. Film scanners are also used to scan colour slides and negatives. The images are converted to digital information and saved as JPEG files. As we have seen in the earlier section on the graphics industry (page 13), JPEGs are a common file format used throughout the industry to save photographs and graphic images. When an image is saved in this format it is compressed to reduce the amount of space it takes up. This is useful for storing or transferring files.

Fig. 2.117 *Using a flatbed scanner*

Image manipulation

Once the photograph is in the computer it can be worked on to create the image required for the design. Poor quality photographs can be enhanced and a range of creative effects can be applied using one of the many image manipulation software packages that are available. Two of the most commonly used are *Paint Shop Pro* and the industry standard package, *Adobe Photoshop*. Both allow images and graphic designs to be created and modified on-screen. Text can be added, colours changed and unwanted backgrounds removed. The finished artwork can be printed on a conventional computer printer or converted to colour separations for four colour process printing.

Fig. 2.118

PRESENTING YOUR DRAWINGS

There is more to producing good design work than the drawings you make. You also have to present your drawings well. The way you present your designs is very important. There will be occasions when you need to 'sell' your ideas to your teacher or to an examiner. In the real world too, designers are often in situations where they have to sell their designs to clients. So, it is all-important to develop your presentation skills as well as your graphic and design skills – your work can be enhanced if presented well, and spoilt if presented badly.

Backgrounds

Sometimes, your presentation drawings will need to be cut out. Airbrush and marker renderings in particular can get very dirty and messy around the edges of the drawings. Cutting them out tidies them up and improves their appearance considerably. Cut-out drawings can be mounted on almost any appropriate background. You can buy ready-made graduated-colour backgrounds in paper and card, or you can produce your own using an airbrush. Streaked backgrounds can be easily made by mixing pastel powder with Clean Art fluid and applying to paper with cotton wool or a piece of lint. Photographs, photocopies and even newspaper can make good backgrounds, if they are relevant to the theme of your work. Use the background to create an effect that will enhance your work. Choose the colours carefully so that the background does not detract from the subject.

Fig. 2.119 *Mounting and presenting your drawings well will improve the look of your work*

Mounting

One way of mounting your work is 'surface mounting', which entails fixing it directly on to a piece of mounting card. Take care to position your work carefully on the mount and leave a slightly larger border at the bottom. This will help to draw the viewer's eye in to the drawing and make it more pleasing to look at. When placing several drawings together on one mount, position them carefully and aim to achieve a balanced layout.

Another method is to use a 'window mount'. This is a mount that has had a hole ('window') cut into it, and your work is positioned behind the card. Window mounts require a little more skill than surface mounts, but are very effective. The window can be cut either with a sharp knife or with a special mount cutter, which you can buy from art shops. It is possible to obtain cutters that will cut circular and elliptical windows. Fig. 2.122 shows the stages involved in making window mounts.

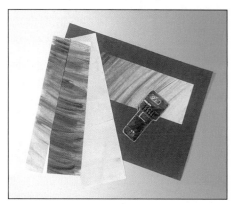

Fig. 2.120 *Examples of graduated and streaked backgrounds*

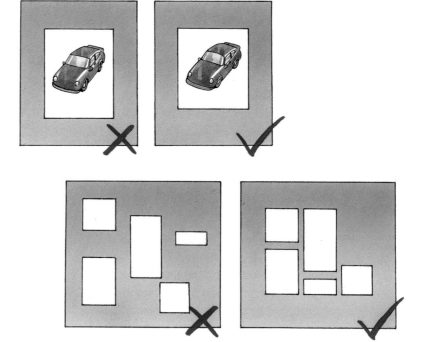

Fig. 2.121 *The way you position your work on mounts is an important consideration*

58

Adhesives for mounting

When fixing your work to mounts, avoid using any glue or adhesive that will make your work too wet. Liquid glues and pastes will cause your drawings to wrinkle, and they may not lie flat when the glue has dried. Spray adhesives such as Spray Mount and Photo Mount are very good for fixing, as they allow the work to be repositioned before drying, but you must use them in a well-ventilated area to avoid breathing in any harmful fumes. Rubber-based adhesives such as Cow Gum are also effective, and have the advantage that any surplus gum can be removed when dry by gently rubbing with your finger or a putty rubber. Adhesive sticks such as Pritt Stick are good for small pieces of work, but they do not always allow for easy repositioning. Work displayed in window mounts is held in position with masking tape or drafting tape.

Dry mounting

Dry mounting is a method of mounting work that involves using a shellac-based tissue (shellac is a type of resin) which becomes sticky when heated. Special, heated dry-mounting presses are often used to mount work in this way, but it can also be done very easily using a domestic iron (take care not to burn yourself when handling a hot iron). The tissue is cut exactly to the shape of the drawing and is 'tacked' to the back of

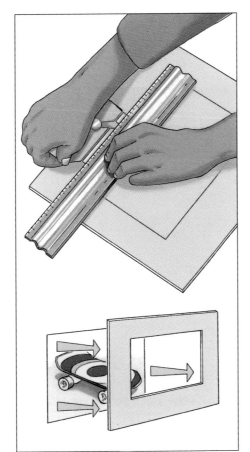

Fig. 2.122 *Stages in window mounting*

the work by touching it with the tip of an iron. The work is then positioned on the mount and covered with heatproof paper, such as brown parcel paper. The iron is put on the brown paper and the work is 'ironed'. The heat from the iron melts the adhesive in the tissue and the pressure of the iron ensures that air is removed and the work is flat.

Protecting your work

A useful way of protecting your work is to cover it with transparent material. Drawings can be sandwiched between clear plastic sheets and then heat sealed. This is known as 'laminating'. Most coloured media can be laminated without damaging them, but it is a good idea to test out a sample first to ensure that your work is not affected by heat.

Another way to protect your work is to attach overlay sheets to it. This can be easily done with most mounted work. A sheet of tracing paper or drafting film is secured to the back of the mount with tape and then folded over the front to protect the drawing. Alternatively, transparent acetate sheets can be stuck to the front of mounted work. First, the acetate sheet is cut to the same size as the mount, then a sheet of paper is placed on the acetate (the paper should be approximately one centimetre smaller than the acetate all the way round). This acts as a mask while the acetate is sprayed with adhesive. The mask is then removed and the acetate is turned over and placed on the work (Fig, 2.124).

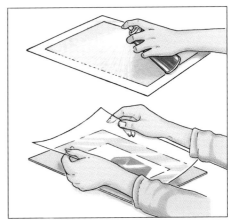

Fig. 2.124 *Protecting a drawing with an acetate overlay*

Some media are affected by prolonged exposure to light. For instance, marker pen work fades if it is left in bright sunlight, and it really needs to be protected either in a drawer or a folder. However, shutting your drawings away is not always practical, particularly if they need to be on display.

Fig. 2.123 *Dry mounting a drawing*

Mike Mowat has over 30 years experience in signs and paintwork. He has run Castle Customs, a successful graphics company situated near Lincoln for the last 14 years.

When he began the company, he specialised in repairing motorcycle fairings and panels by plastic welding. Once the repairs were complete he needed to replace the graphics on them, so instead of buying signs, he invested in the equipment to produce his own.

The production of graphic signs was so successful that it grew into a second business which specialises in vehicle livery, graphics and signs for racing cars and motorcycles and even lettering for aircraft.

CADCAM

Computer aided design and **computer aided manufacture** is used extensively in the graphics industry, from page layout and graphic design to packaging (see page 61) and sign making. Many applications used in industry can be used in school for Graphic Products projects.

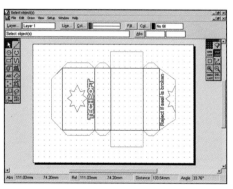

Fig. 2.125

Desktop publishing

Page design for leaflets, brochures and books is done using sophisticated desktop publishing software such as *Adobe Pagemaker* or *QuarkXpress*. Professional software such as this is often too expensive for use in school, but good results in project work can be obtained with familiar software such as *Microsoft Word* and *Microsoft Publisher*. Modern word processing software packages can be used to produce pages for your project folders and can be used to make prototypes of your products such as leaflets and brochures. Photographs, saved as JPEGs, can be imported and lettering and text added.

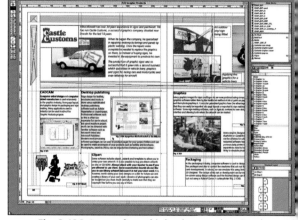

Fig. 2.126 *A page from this book created on QuarkXpress*

Clipart

Some software includes clipart, wizards and templates to allow you to create your own artwork. It is also possible to buy pre-drawn artwork on disc or CD-ROM. *Always check with your teacher to see if you are allowed to use them. Some examination boards do not like you to use library artwork because it is not your own work.* It is, however, worth saving your own designs on a disk for future use and creating a library of your own work. Libraries of photographs can also be bought but you must check carefully to make sure that they are copyright free before you use any of them.

Fig. 2.127 *Clipart*

An outdoor vinyl sign being fitted.

Applying the graphics for a vehicle livery

Mike has produced graphics for some of the top motorcycle racing teams including the Virgin Mobile Yamaha Team in 2000

Graphics

Many graphics images for signs and logos etc are now produced using computer graphics software rather than by the traditional method of ink or paint on paper and then photographing it. Computer generated graphics have the advantage that they can easily be imported into page layouts or exported to sign making software. Some sign making software, such as *SignLab*, contains its own design interface and drawing tools where the artwork can be created.

Fig. 2.128

Fig. 2.129

Many graphic designers work with industrial software such as *Adobe Illustrator* or *CorelDRAW* to create graphics. More than adequate results can be obtained in school using the drawing tools in *Microsoft Word*. Industrial software has advantages when artwork needs to be professionally printed using the four colour process and colour separations need to be made (see page 15). In school, where you are likely to simulate production using an ink jet printer, this is not necessary.

Packaging

In the packaging industry, computer software is used to design the packages and also to control the machines that cut out the card developments. In school, we can simulate this using *Techsoft 2D Designer*. The design of the net or development can be made on-screen using design software and the finished design can be cut out using a *Roland Camm 1 cutter-plotter* (Fig. 2.130).

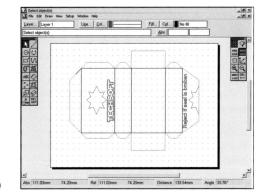

Fig. 2.130

61

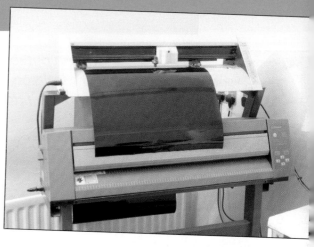

SignLab is used in industry to design signs which are then printed or cut out on self adhesive vinyl sheet.

Roland Camm computer aided cutters and engraving machines are used extensively in industry.

Castle Customs use SignLab, an industry standard piece of software for their sign design and manufacture. The customer's design can be created on-screen or scanned in from paper artwork. SignLab is then used to design the sign. It is cut out using a Roland Camm 1 cutter plotter, which is very similar to the ones used in school.

CADCAM can be used effectively for the manufacture of graphic products in school in the same way as it is used in industry. The *Roland Camm 1* cutter is a very useful piece of equipment for making developments and boxes in card, as well as vinyl signs.

Fig. 2.131

3D developments in card

Fig. 2.132

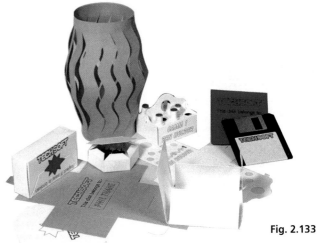

Fig. 2.133

Developments for package designs like the one shown in Fig. 2.132 can be created using CAD software such as Techsoft Design Tools and then cut out using the Camm 1 computer controlled cutter (Fig. 2.131). In the packaging

industry, designs such as this would be die cut by pressing a cutter through the card. In school, this industrial process is simulated using the cutter and the batch production of a product is still possible.

Fig. 2.133 shows some examples of products manufactured in this way. Using the Techsoft software, it is possible to print your graphic design onto the card before cutting it out.

In addition to traditional vinyl signs, Castle Customs are able to digitally print photographs onto vinyl material using a Roland Camm digital printer (shown on the left).

Vinyl signs have a life of between 5 and 7 years depending on the quality of vinyl used. To provide support and allow them to be fitted to walls, they are mounted on a PVC board such as 'forex' or 'foamalux'.

The photograph on the right shows how an image can be digitally printed onto self adhesive vinyl and used as part of a vehicle livery.

Vinyl signs

Vinyl signs can be made in school using a computer controlled cutter in exactly the same way as Mike Mowat manufactures them at Castle Customs in the case study above.

Fig. 2.134 *The sign design*

The sign is designed on-screen using either Techsoft Design tools or SignLab. It is possible to scan logos or artwork for signs, but because scanned images are bitmaps (i.e. made from dots or pixels), they have to be converted to vector images before they can be cut out. Vector images consist of lines, rather than dots, which the cutter can follow. SignLab has its own vectoring facility, but you will need to use a piece of vectoring software before you can cut out your scanned design with Techsoft.

The sign is cut from self adhesive vinyl sheet using the Camm 1 cutter. The cutter is set up so that the cutting blade cuts only through the vinyl sheet and not through the paper backing.

Fig. 2.135 *The sign being cut*

Once the sign is cut, the unwanted vinyl is removed by lifting it away from the letters. This process is known as **'weeding'** and must be carried out carefully so that delicate parts of the letters or logos are not damaged.

Fig. 2.136 *The sign being 'weeded'*

When the sign has been weeded, a special low tack application tape is stuck over the sign. The backing paper can be removed and the sign is held in place by the tape until it is applied.

Fig. 2.137

The sign can be positioned and held in place by the application. Once in the correct position, the sign is pressed down firmly, air bubbles are removed using a soft plastic squeegee and the application tape is removed.

Fig. 2.138

63

Putting it into practice

1 Make a tonal range for your pencil.

Do this by shading very lightly and gradually increasing the pressure until you have the full range of the tone or shading that the pencil can produce.

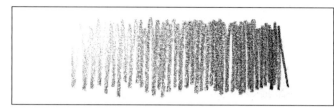

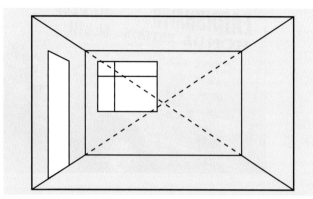

2 Spend a few moments working through the exercises on page 26. Use them as warm up exercises each time you begin drawing.

3 Working freehand, draw a circle and then an ellipse. Don't forget to construct a frame first and then draw the shape within it, touching the sides.

4 Choose a variety of objects from around the room and make freehand objects of them. Begin by drawing crates and then draw the objects inside them.

5 Make a single-point perspective drawing of the interior of your bedroom, similar to the one shown above.

6 Draw four cubes in perspective and render them to represent glass, concrete, plastic and metal.

7 Choose a colour and, using poster paint or gouache, produce a tonal range for that colour by adding black and white.

8 Copy the camera shown above and render it using a variety of different textures.

9 Copy the colour wheel shown on the right and, using only three colours, colour in the primary, secondary and tertiary colours. Mix all the colours from the three primary colours.

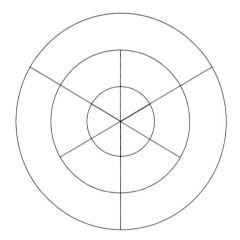

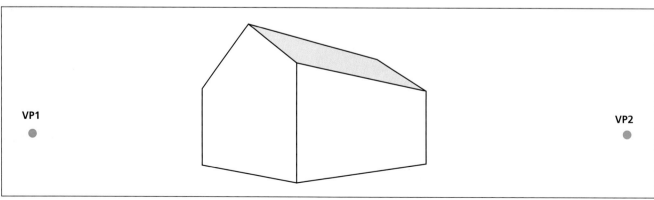

10 Copy the two-point perspective drawing of the house shown above and add the following features: two windows, a door and a chimney. Make sure that you use the vanishing points to construct the drawing.

3· Geometrical and technical drawing

Geometrical Drawing

Geometrical drawing allows us to construct shapes and forms accurately. It is very useful when constructing 3-dimensional forms to be developed from sheet materials. Geometric drawing is also used in developing ideas when modelling and prototyping as shown on pages 92 and 93.

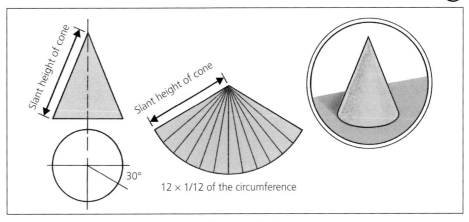

Fig. 3.1 *A cone constructed using geometric drawing techniques*

Fig. 3.2 *An example of a technical drawing*

Technical Drawing

Technical drawings are used to show how to make things that have been designed. They are used to give precise information, such as exact shape and size and the materials to be used, to realise the design. Technical drawings must be accurate and precise so that what is shown in the drawing can be clearly understood and made. It is important to remember that other people as well as yourself, need to be able to understand what you have drawn, especially if they are going to help you make what you have designed. Well thought out drawing will lead to straightforward, problem-free making. Technical drawing is an important part of the design process, and it allows the designer to finalise construction details and check important measurements before making begins.

Drawing instruments and equipment

Because a high level of accuracy is required for technical drawing, you will need to use appropriate drawing instruments and equipment to enable you to work precisely. Freehand drawing techniques are not suitable for this type of work.

Technical drawings are traditionally made on cartridge paper or tracing paper, which is securely held on a drawing board to prevent it moving while the drawing is being made. Some drawing boards require the paper to be held with spring clips or tape while some plastic drawing boards have their own built-in paper clamping device.

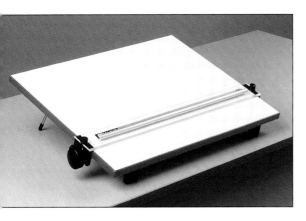

Fig. 3.3 *A plastic drawing board with a parallel motion*

When working on a drawing board, horizontal lines are drawn using a special ruler known as a parallel motion. The parallel motion slides up and down the board while remaining parallel to the top and bottom edge of the board.

Computer aided design software can be used to create working drawings which are then printed on an ink jet printer or drawn using a pen plotter. Software such as *ProDesktop* can generate working drawings very easily from 3D computer models.

Fig. 3.4 *A drawing board with a rack and pinion system to control the parallel motion*

65

At AESSEAL plc technical drawing is a very important part of the designing process. The design engineers use a range of drawing-office equipment, similar to that available in schools for technical drawing. Using such equipment helps the design engineer to draw to the degree of accuracy and precision that is vital to ensure that what is shown in the drawing can be clearly understood and go on to be made.

The drawing on the right is of a journal/thrust bearing from a turbocharger, it shows the size of the component and the material to be used – this particular component is made from an alloy of 94 per cent aluminium and 6 per cent tin. Many mechanical systems such as pumps contain rotating parts that have to be sealed. This is

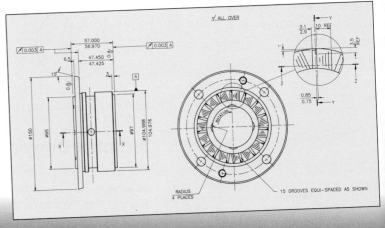

Set squares

Set squares are one of the most useful drawing aids for technical drawing. They are transparent plastic triangles which, when held firmly against a tee square or parallel motion, can be used to draw lines at angles. For most of your work, you will need two set squares, a 30/60 degree square and a 45 degree square. The basic angles that can be obtained with set squares are 90, 60, 45 and 30 degrees, but other angles can be drawn by placing squares edge to edge on the paper. For example, a line can be drawn at 75 degrees by placing a 30 degree square next to the 45 degree one, and so on (Fig. 3.5). Adjustable set squares are also available (as the name suggests, they can be adjusted and set at the angle you require).

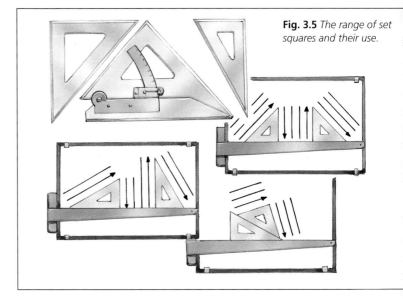

Fig. 3.5 *The range of set squares and their use.*

Protractors

Protractors are used for measuring and constructing angles. They are made of transparent plastic and are marked in degrees. The most commonly used protractors are marked from 0 to 180 degrees, but there are also circular ones, which measure up to 360 degrees (Fig. 3.6).

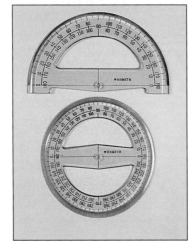

Fig. 3.6

Curves

There is a variety of drawing instruments that you can use to draw curved lines. French curves are made of plastic and are available in a variety of curved shapes which can be drawn around. A 'flexi-curve' is a flexible strip of plastic that can be bent to any shape of curve. Flexi-curves are constructed with a lead and spring steel core which allows them to be bent and re-bent as required.

Fig. 3.7 *French curves and a flexi-curve*

A seal used in food product mixing machines

to prevent liquids and gases leaking within the system or escaping into the environment. The liquids and gases concerned may be under high pressure and they may also be dangerously toxic or corrosive.

The manufacture of mechanical seals for such systems is a highly developed and precise engineering activity. AESSEAL plc specialise in the manufacture of many types of mechanical seals used throughout the world. Their business is built around customer service and the aim is to deliver any standard product anywhere within 48 hours. If a large pumping system for oil or gas supplies or for chemical processing fails then speed is essential.

A key to the success of AESSEAL has been their investment in new technology. CAD/CAM systems mean that products can be manufactured 4 times faster than they could 5 years ago and cheaper than they were 18 years ago.

Templates

Templates are often used as guides for drawing shapes. When making technical drawings they can save you a lot of time. Templates are usually made of plastic, in different shapes or with shapes cut out which can be drawn around. There is a vast range of shapes available, from simple circles and ellipses to symbols and human figures.

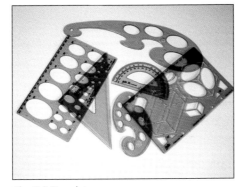

Fig. 3.8 *Templates*

A pair of compasses

A pair of compasses are mostly used for drawing circles and arcs, but they can also be used for constructing shapes, and dividing lines and angles. There are many types (Fig. 3.9), but the best ones for technical drawing are the spring

bow type, which are adjusted by a screw mechanism and once set do not slip. Large circles are drawn with beam compasses, where the centre point and the pencil are adjusted and then locked on to a bar or beam.

Cleaning equipment

Drawing instruments and drafting aids must be kept clean or they will dirty your drawings. Tee squares, parallel motions, set squares and templates should all be cleaned regularly. You can do this with one of the special art cleaners that are available or lighter fuel. Always remember to take great care when using flammable liquids and observe the special safety instructions on the container. Cleaning with soapy water is an alternative, but it is often messy and not always convenient. Drawings can be cleaned up with a paper cleaner or a putty rubber.

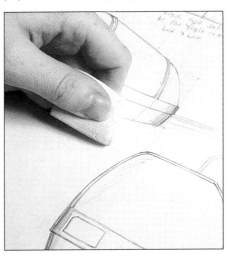

Fig. 3.10 *A putty rubber being used to clean up a drawing*

Fig. 3.9 *A range of compasses*

67

The AESSEAL factory headquarters site in Rotherham is linked to the companies 10 internationally located servers. 3D CAD systems used to generate designs can therefore draw upon one of the worlds most comprehensive databases within the engineering seal industry.

3D CAD drawing

Many engineering designers have moved to 3D CAD systems that enable them to view their designs from many angles without moving from the drawing that they are working on. 3D CAD systems also link to PDM (process data management) software to allow designs to develop with continual reference to how the product will be manufactured. This process makes best potential use of the manufacturing capability available even before the design stage is complete. The advantage of PDM is to improve manufacturing efficiency and reduce costs.

LINES

In technical drawing, different types of lines mean different things. The British Standards Institution publish documents which show how they should be drawn.

Fig. 3.11 *(right) Some of the lines used in technical drawing*

1

CONTINUOUS THICK – Visible outlines and edges

2

CONTINUOUS THIN – Dimension lines, projection lines, hatching and outlines of adjacent parts

3

THIN DASHES – Hidden outlines and edges

4

THIN, LONG CHAIN – Centre lines

Fig. 3.12 *Uses of line*

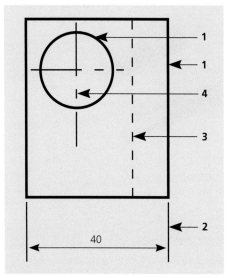

Two thicknesses of line are used (thick lines should be twice the width of thin lines). It is normal practice to plan and draft drawings with thin 'construction' lines using a fairly hard pencil such as a 2H, and then go over the outline of objects with thick lines using a softer pencil such as an H or HB. The diagram in Fig. 3.12 shows how the different types of line are used.

You can make technical drawings in either pencil or ink, but it is important not to mix the two. It is easier when working in ink to maintain the line thicknesses. Use a fine pen for the thin lines and a pen with a tip that is twice as wide for thick lines. All the lines in a drawing should be uniformly dense and bold.

AESSEAL also use Computer Aided Analysis software to simulate seal performance. This helps to increase the reliability of prototypes and reduce research and development time.

Computer Aided Analysis

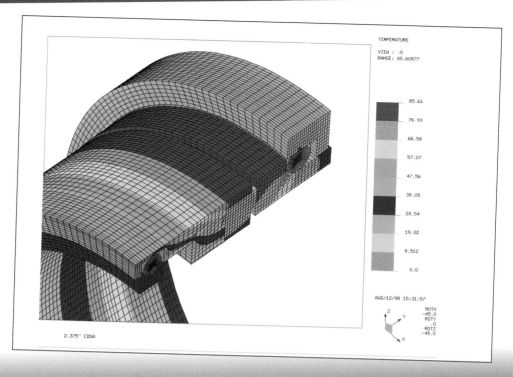

DIMENSIONING

All working drawings, except assembly drawings, need to be dimensioned in order to show what size the object is in real life. The rules for dimensioning are clearly set out in both BSI booklets (BS308 and PP 8888/1). Some of the main points are listed below.

1 Dimensions should be written on the drawing so that the measurements are the right way up when reading from the bottom or from the right-hand side of the drawing.

2 Projection lines and dimension lines should be drawn outside the outline of the drawing whenever possible.

3 Smaller measurements should be written closer to the drawing.

4 Dimensions should be shown in millimetres. The symbol for millimetres (mm) does not have to be written on each dimension, as long as the drawing is clearly labelled to show that all dimensions are shown in millimetres.

5 The dimension should be written centrally above the dimension line.

6 Dimensions should not be repeated or used any more than necessary.

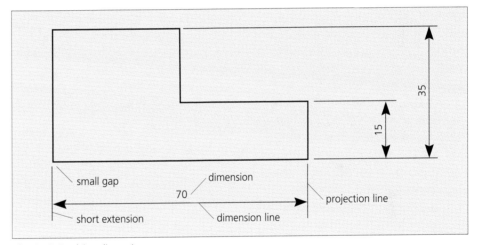

Fig. 3.13 *Applying dimensions*

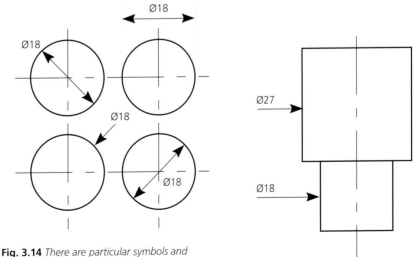

Fig. 3.14 *There are particular symbols and various ways to dimension diameters*

69

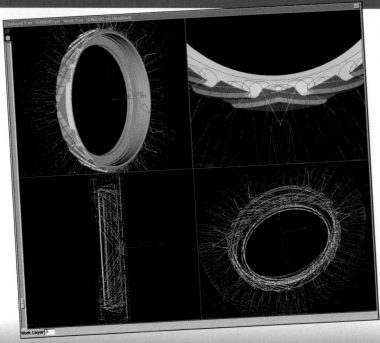

CAM programming is part of the integrated 3D CAD/CAM system. The photograph on the right shows, in three dimensions, the machine tool cutting path for the manufacture of a seal component.

CAM programming.

USING INFORMATION AND COMMUNICATION TECHNOLOGY

Technical drawings are often made using information and communication technology (ICT). ICT enables you to create drawings on the computer screen, save them to the computer's memory, on to a disk or CD-ROM and then print them out on to paper later. There are many advantages to working this way. For instance, drawings do not have to be redrawn completely when alterations are made – all you have to do is retrieve your original drawing from where you saved it and then carry out the necessary changes. Drawings produced in this way also have the advantage that they can be e-mailed to clients or manufacturers.

Storing drawings is easy and efficient. Large drawings take up less space on a disk than they do in a plan chest or folder. Libraries of frequently used symbols or components can be built up and used in a drawing whenever required.

Computer images for technical drawings are produced using a process called 'vector drawing'. A vector is a line that has a particular size and direction, and the drawing is plotted as a series of points joined with straight lines. Even circles are drawn in this way. Computer graphics software speeds up the drawing process by allowing lines to be repeated or redrawn as required. Dimensioning is also made easy – arrows can be automatically put on the end of dimension lines and measurements can be added to the drawing according to whatever national or international standard has been preset. Images can be enlarged, reduced, rotated or flipped simply by selecting an option shown on the screen.

3D solid modelling

The more traditional drawing software such as *AutoCAD* or *EasiCAD* require you to make a drawing on-screen but more modern packages such as *ProDESKTOP* and *ProENGINEER* allow to create a 3-dimensional solid model on-screen. The model is then imported into the software's drawing interface and the technical drawings are automatically produced from the 3D models data. All you have to do is arrange the drawing as you want it and add any extra notes or dimensions that you require. This type of software will also produce a 3D rendered view of your product of near photographic quality.

Fig. 3.15 *A computer generated technical drawing*

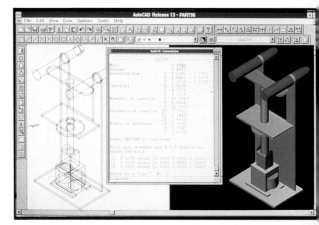

Fig. 3.16 *A computer generated technical drawing with a 3D solid model*

The tool path can then be fully animated within the software using 'Machine Tool Verification' to give a better insight into any potential problems that might occur during manufacture. All of these processes combine to reduce overall time and increase the efficiency of the expensive machining processes.

Machine Tool Verification.

Software packages make drawing easier, but they do not take away the need to be able to understand and read technical drawings. The computer only *aids* the drawing process – you still need to plan and think carefully about the drawing yourself. The computer will not do it for you.

Inputting information

When you use a computer for making drawings, you need to feed information into it so that it knows what you want to draw. This information is input using a variety of devices. You can draw directly on-screen in the normal way using a mouse or a graphics tablet, which is a device that senses the pressure while you are drawing and feeds information to a 'puck' on screen to accurately reproduce the drawing.

Fig. 3.18 *A graphics tablet*

Fig. 3.17 *Drawing directly on the screen using a mouse*

Producing 'hard copy'

In some manufacturing processes, products are made directly from a 3D computer model and hard copy is not required. When needed, drawings made on a computer are not printed out on to paper until they are finally complete and ready for use. The printed drawings are known as 'hard copy'. Most modern ink-jet printers are capable of producing the detail needed for technical drawings. Small drawings (e.g. A4 and A3 size) can be printed very successfully on both ink-jet and laser printers. Larger drawings are best printed out using a plotter. This is a device which draws the image with a pen. Small plotters are usually the 'flatbed' type with the pen held by a moving arm. In industry, larger 'roller bed' plotters are most likely to be used. Drawings can be printed on to paper, card, tracing paper, drafting film or even plastic sheet.

Fig. 3.19 *An A3 size drawing being printed*

Fig. 3.20 *Using an A3 plotter*

Fig. 3.21 *A large roller bed plotter in use*

The machining programmes are sent electronically direct to CNC machine tools located in many different manufacturing sites. The programmes are then automatically uploaded into the machines to begin machining. The machine tools usually operate unmanned throughout the night and into weekends in order to remain cost effective.

STANDARDISING DRAWINGS

In industry the person who has made the drawing very rarely actually makes the product that has been drawn. Component parts of a product are often made in different countries and brought together for assembly. It is, therefore, essential that drawings which are to be used as instructions to make things can be easily understood by those who use them – **misinterpretation of a working drawing could prove to be very expensive for a manufacturer**. In order to overcome this, drawings made in Britain are produced to British Standards. These have been set out by the British Standards Institution (BSI) and provide a set of rules on how drawings are to be done. The rules appear in a booklet known as *BS 308*. Schools and colleges often work to an abbreviated edition of this, known as *PP 8888/1 2001, Engineering Drawing Practice For Schools and Colleges*. The examples provided here are taken from this booklet. The British Standard provides a 'language' of drawing which is easily understood by designers and manufacturers. The same standards apply to all working drawings, regardless of whether they are produced on computer or by hand on a drawing board.

Fig. 3.22 *British Standards Institution booklets*

Layout

PP 8888/1 includes rules on how to set out a drawing. A **title block** should be included at the bottom of the sheet or on the lower right-hand side. This block should contain the information required to enable the drawing to be understood. Your name and the date need to be included in the block, along with a symbol to show the form of projection you have used (projection is dealt with later in this chapter), the scale used, the title of the drawing and the drawing number.

Drawings are made in either **portrait** format or **landscape** format. Portrait is when the longest side of the drawing is vertical (the shape normally used when painting portraits) and landscape when the longest side is horizontal (the shape normally used when painting landscapes).

Fig. 3.24 *Portrait and landscape drawing formats*

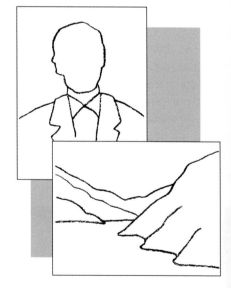

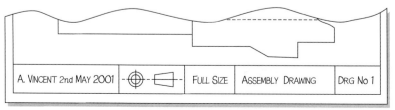

Fig. 3.23 *A typical title block*

The photographs show some of the multi-axes and multi-spindle machines used at the AESSEAL Rotherham site.

The final stage of the process is testing to ensure that quality control is maintained. The testing and the analysis of test results are also computer controlled processes.

Seal testing rig

Scales

Drawings of objects that would fit on to the paper are known as 'full size' (they are drawn to a scale of 1:1). However, the objects you draw will not always fit easily on to the paper. If an object is too large you will need to draw it smaller than its real size, using a reduction scale e.g. an object drawn half its actual size is drawn to a scale of 1:2).

The reduction scales recommended by the British Standards Institution are

1:2, 1:5, 1:10, 1:20, 1:50, 1:100, 1:200, 1:500 and 1:1000. If an object is too small for the details to be seen, you will need to draw a larger version, using an enlargement scale. Sometimes only part of an object needs to be enlarged and is shown in a separate view on the same drawing. The recommended enlargement scales are 2:1, 5:1, 10:1, 20:1 and 50:1.

Fig. 3.26

The scale you use depends on the size of the paper available and the size of the object you are drawing. You should always use a scale that allows information to be easily and clearly seen. Also, the scale used should always be stated clearly on the drawing in order to avoid misunderstandings. Without a scale indicated, the house in the drawing in Fig. 3.26 could be a doll's house or a real house!

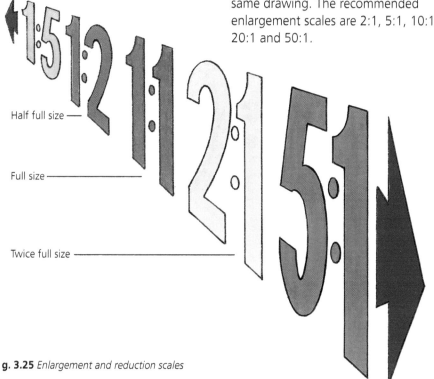

Half full size

Full size

Twice full size

Fig. 3.25 *Enlargement and reduction scales*

ORTHOGRAPHIC PROJECTION

Orthographic projection is a method of showing 3-dimensional objects in 2-dimensional drawings. The objects are drawn from three different views, known as the plan (the view from the top), front elevation (from the front) and end elevation (from the side). Orthographic projection is used in most working drawings of 3-dimensional objects.

In terms of geometry, orthographic drawing uses two planes of projection – the horizontal and the vertical plane. The object is drawn as if it is projected on to these planes. The planes intersect as shown in Fig. 3.27, producing four quadrants (angles). Imagine that the object to be drawn is placed in one of the quadrants and the views projected on to the planes.

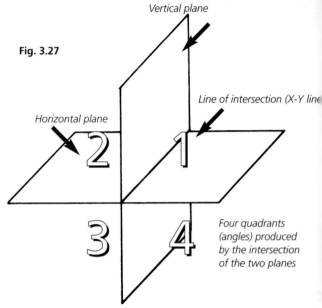

Fig. 3.27

Four quadrants (angles) produced by the intersection of the two planes

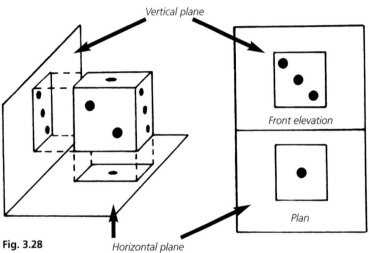

Fig. 3.28

Although four quadrants are produced by the intersection of the two planes, only the first and third are used in orthographic drawing. This is because the views in the second and fourth angles overlap and would be difficult to draw and interpret clearly.

The drawings in Fig. 3.28 show a dice which has been drawn in the first angle. The front elevation is projected through the dice (i.e. ignoring the rest of the dice) against the vertical plane and the plan is projected against the horizontal plane. The drawing is then made as if the two views are folded flat at the intersection of the two planes to create one drawing with two views of the dice.

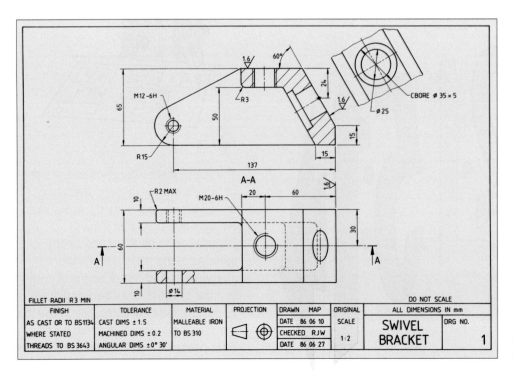

Drawings of objects in the third angle are made in a similar way, except that the drawing shows what you would see if you looked through the vertical and horizontal planes at the object. Third angle projection was originally used in North America and is sometimes called 'American Projection'. It is becoming more widely used in Europe and may well become the international standard.

Fig. 3.29 *An example of a first angle orthographic drawing*

74

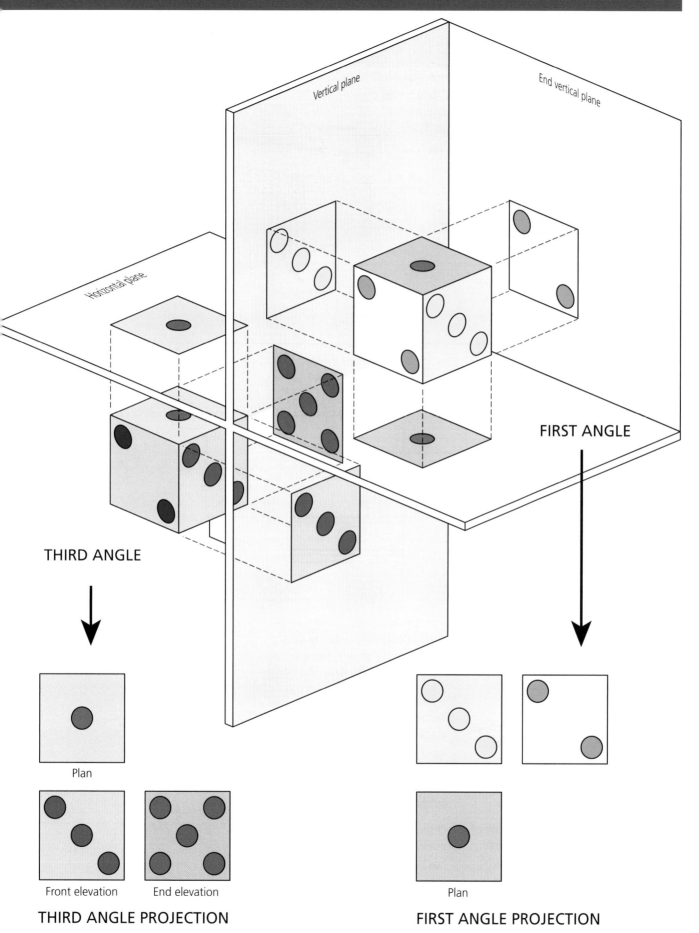

Vertical plane

End vertical plane

Horizontal plane

FIRST ANGLE

THIRD ANGLE

Plan

Front elevation

End elevation

THIRD ANGLE PROJECTION

Plan

FIRST ANGLE PROJECTION

g. 3.30 *First and third angle orthographic drawing*

FIRST ANGLE PROJECTION

The illustration in Fig. 3.31 shows a pencil sharpener with arrows indicating the position of views to be drawn in first angle orthographic projection. You will see that, though they are not all indicated, there are six possible views that could be drawn if necessary. However, only three or four views are usually drawn, depending upon the details that need to be shown. When making a first angle drawing, always begin with the front elevation because that will determine the layout of the rest of the drawing. Some objects do not have an obvious front elevation so you will just have to choose one to work from. Position the front elevation on a faintly drawn line which represents the X–Y line of the quadrant.

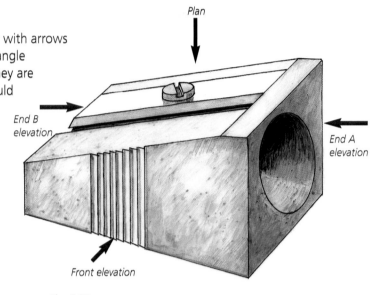

Fig. 3.31

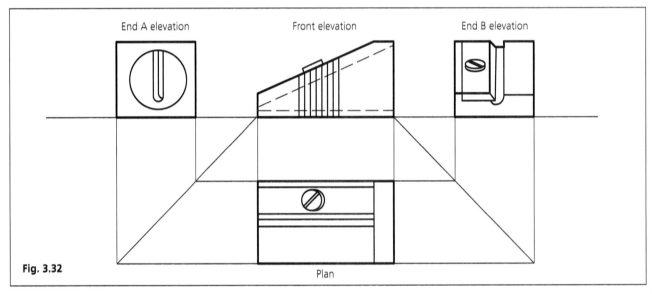

Fig. 3.32

Next, draw elevation A, as shown by the direction of the arrow in the diagram. In first angle projection, this elevation is projected through the object, as represented by the front elevation, and drawn on the left-hand side of the page. This can be seen in Fig. 3.32. The same principle applies to end elevation B, which is drawn on the right-hand side of the page. Position each end elevation the same distance away from the front elevation. At the two bottom corners of the front elevation, draw a line at 45°. These lines will enable you to position and construct the plan view. Project the vertical lines of the end elevations down until they meet the 45° lines. From the point where they meet the line continue

them horizontally with the parallel motion or tee square. You can then project the vertical lines of the front elevation down and construct the plan.

Remember, all the work you do at this stage is construction work and should be drawn faintly with a 2H pencil. Once you are happy with your drawing, you can go over the main outlines with a softer, darker pencil such as an HB.

Orthographic drawings need to be clearly marked to show which type of projection has been used. There are standard symbols for this. They are shown in Fig. 3.33. The symbols themselves are examples of orthographic drawing. They are front and end elevations of a truncated cone shown

in either first or third angle. The first angle symbol shows the end elevation projected to the right of the front elevation. The third angle symbol shows it in its true position to the left of the front elevation.

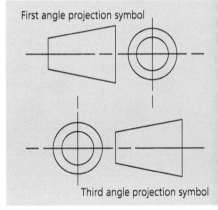

Fig. 3.33

76

THIRD ANGLE PROJECTION

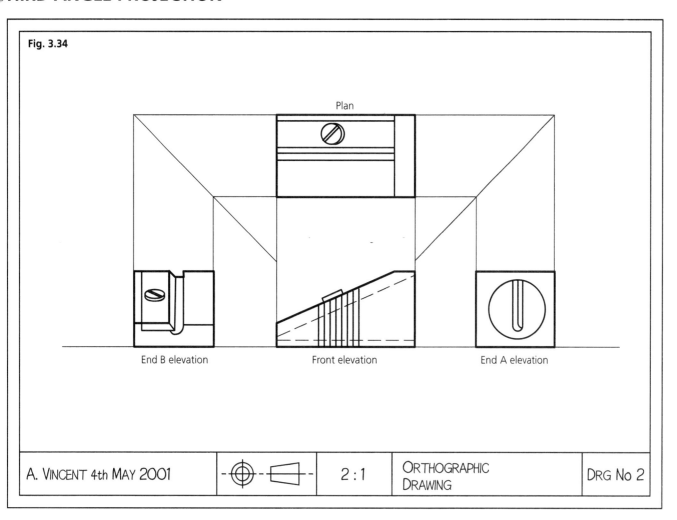

Fig. 3.34

Plan

End B elevation

Front elevation

End A elevation

A. Vincent 4th May 2001 | 2:1 | Orthographic Drawing | DRG No 2

The same pencil sharpener has been drawn in Fig. 3.34. However, this time it has been drawn using third angle projection (you will see that the third angle symbol has been included in the title block). You will notice that, unlike first angle drawing, the plan view is positioned directly above the front elevation, and the end elevations are placed on the side nearest their true position. This makes third angle drawings easier to draw and much simpler to read and understand than first angle drawings. There is no need to worry about having to project the views through the object – they simply open out from the front elevation. The increasing popularity of third angle projection is probably due to its clarity – you can simply ask yourself, 'If I stand here, what will I see?'.

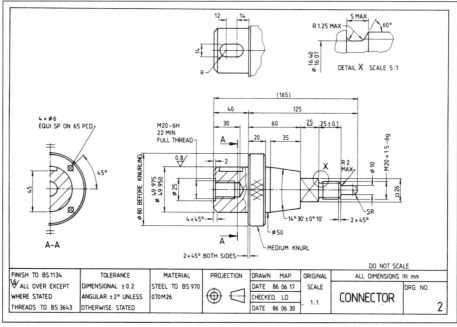

Fig. 3.35 *An example of a third angle drawing*

SECTIONS

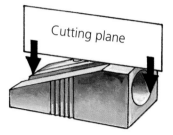

Fig. 3.36

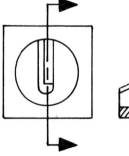

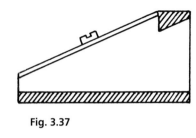

Fig. 3.37

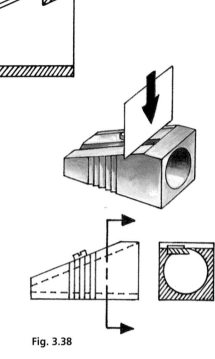

Fig. 3.38

There may be a time when you need to show the inside of an object and dashed lines would not allow you to show sufficient hidden detail. In such a case you would need to draw a sectional view. Fig. 3.36 shows the pencil sharpener about to be cut lengthways by an imaginary cutting plane. The cut-off part of the sharpener nearest the viewer is 'discarded' and then the cross-section of the remainder is drawn in detail. The parts of the object that are 'cut' are hatched with 45 degree lines, as shown in Fig. 3.38.

The line with two arrows drawn on the end elevation in Fig. 3.37 represents the cutting plane. The arrows show which part of the drawing is retained. Sectional views are often incorporated into orthographic drawings in order to make them clearer.

Fig. 3.38 shows another sectional view through the pencil sharpener. In this case the line representing the cutting plane is drawn on the front elevation with the arrows indicating which part of the view is to be retained.

Assembly drawings

Most of the things that you are likely to design and make will consist of more than one part. The individual components are usually shown on a parts drawing or a detail drawing, using orthographic projection. At some stage however, you will be required to show how the parts fit together to form the complete object. Drawings that show us how to do this are called '**assembly drawings**'. The style of assembly

drawings varies according to what you are designing and making. Sometimes a formal orthographic drawing of the assembled object is made, while on other occasions isometric or perspective drawing might be used.

Sections or part sections are normally used in assembly drawings.

Fig. 3.40 shows a sectional view of a car differential (final drive unit) used in a workshop manual to show how the various parts are assembled.

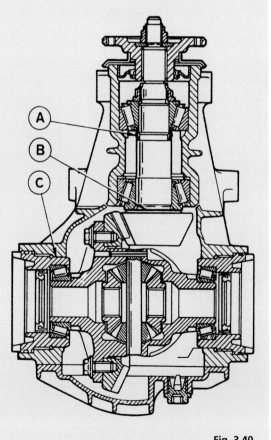

Fig. 3.40

Fig. 3.39 *Example of a part-sectioned assembly drawing*

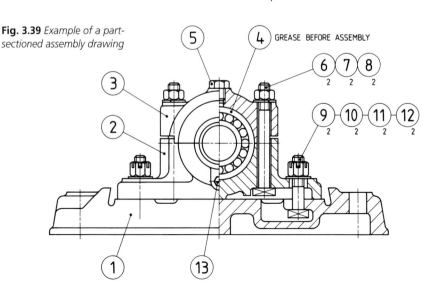

ABBREVIATIONS AND CONVENTIONS

Often there is not enough space on a drawing to write or draw everything in full. If this is the case, you can use standard abbreviations and conventions that have been developed by the BSI.

Abbreviations

Some of the more common abbreviations are listed in Fig. 3.41. You can save a considerable amount of time if you use abbreviations. Check the BSI documents yourself for other abbreviations which may be useful.

Across flats (on head of nut or bolt)	A/F
Centre line	C, CL or c
Computer-aided design	CAD
Computer-aided manufacture	CAM
Centimetre	cm
Centres	CRS
Counterbore	C'BORE
Countersunk	CSK
Countersunk head	CSK HD
Diameter (before a dimension)	Ø
Diameter (in a note)	DIA
Drawing	DRG
External	EXT
Hexagon	HEX
Hexagonal head	HEX HD
Inside diameter	I/D
Internal	INT
Left hand	LH
Material	MATL
Metre	m
Millimetre	mm
Not to scale	NTS
Outside diameter	O/D
Radius (before a dimension)	R
Radius (in a note)	RAD
Right hand	RH
Vanishing point	VP

Fig. 3.41 *Common abbreviations*

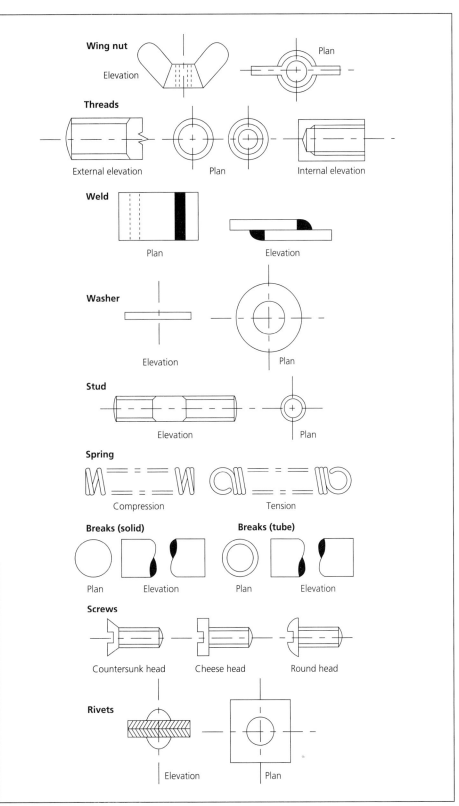

Fig. 3.42 *Some of the standard engineering conventions*

Conventions

There are also standard graphic abbreviations, known as '**conventions**'. A selection of these is shown above in Fig. 3.42 It would be very time consuming, for instance, to have to draw every thread on a bolt – it's far easier to draw its convention. Some computer software packages include these conventions in their clip art libraries.

GEOMETRICAL DRAWING

There are two forms of geometrical drawing: **plane geometry**, which deals with constructing lines, angles and shapes in 2-dimensions, and **solid geometry**, which is used to construct 3-dimensional objects such as cylinders, cones, prisms and pyramids. Solid geometry is dealt with in the modelling section of this book on pages 92 and 93.

In order to construct lines, angles and shapes, we need to have a basic understanding of the terms and shapes used in plane geometry. The basic components of geometrical drawing are shown here in Fig. 3.43. In order to construct them you will need to use the drawing instruments shown on pages 66 and 67.

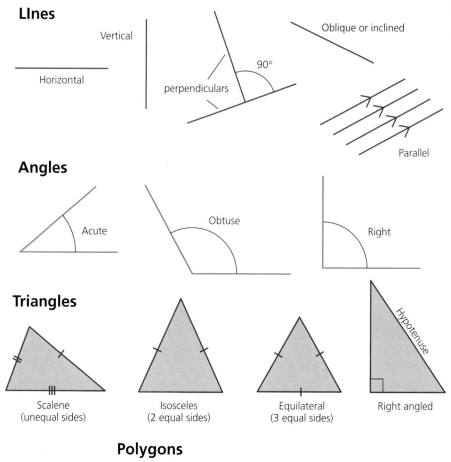

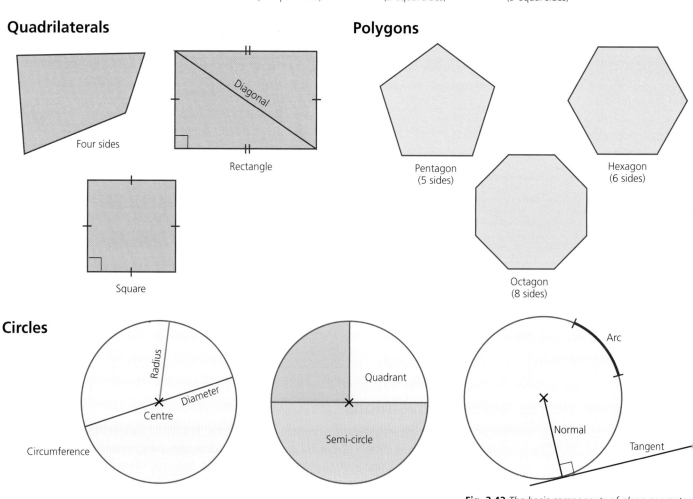

Fig. 3.43 *The basic components of plane geometry*

80

CONSTRUCTIONS USING PLANE GEOMETRY

The following commonly used constructions will be useful to you in both your practical work and in preparation for your GCSE examination.

Bisecting lines

To bisect or divide a line into two equal parts.

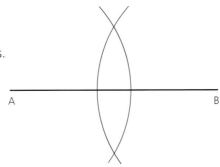
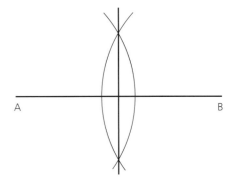

Fig. 3.44 *Bisecting lines*

1. To bisect line AB, set the radius of a pair of compasses to just over half the length of the line.

2. Place the point of a pair of compasses at the end of the line at A and draw an arc. Repeat this at point B

3. Connect the points where the arcs intersect with a line to bisect line AB

Perpendiculars

The same method as above can be used to construct lines which are perpendicular (i.e. at right-angles to each other).

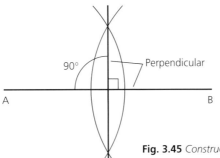

Fig. 3.45 *Constructing perpendicular lines*

Dividing a line

Geometry can also be used to divide a line into a number of equal parts. For example to divide line AB into 7 equal parts.

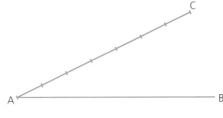
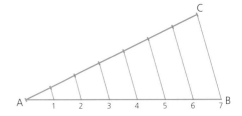

Fig. 3.46 *Dividing a line*

1. Draw line AB

2. Draw line AC. Make the line a length that can easily be divided by the required number.

3. Draw line CB. Place a ruler under the set square to allow parallel lines to be drawn as shown.

Bisecting angles

Use the following construction to bisect angle ABC.

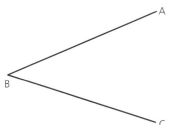
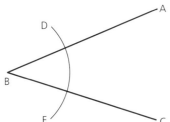
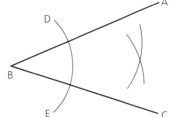
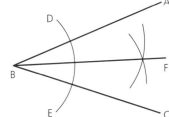

Fig. 3.47 *Bisecting angles*

1. Draw an arc to intersect line AB at D and line CB at E.

2. Place the point of a pair of compasses at the intersection of line AB and draw an arc. Repeat for line CB.

3. Where the arcs intersect (F), draw a line to B to bisect the angle.

CONSTRUCTING SHAPES

Constructing geometric shapes can be useful in graphics projects, especially when designing logos and trademarks. The design for the MG logo (Fig. 3.48) was made by constructing an octagon to enclose the letters. Many logos use similar shapes which are combined with companies' names or trade marks.

Fig. 3.48 *The MG logo*

Constructing regular polygons

The shape of the MG logo is a regular polygon. The diagram in Fig. 3.49 shows a method of constructing regular polygons from a given side.

Follow these stages to construct a regular polygon.

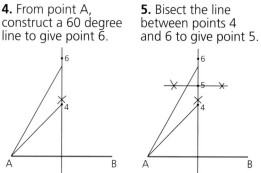

Fig. 3.49

1. Begin by drawing the side AB.

2. Bisect the side AB.

3. From point A, construct a 45 degree line to give point 4

4. From point A, construct a 60 degree line to give point 6.

5. Bisect the line between points 4 and 6 to give point 5.

6. Mark off the distance between points 5 and 6 with a pair of compasses or dividers to give points 7 and 8.

7. Using the line between point 4 and A as a radius, draw a circle using point 4 as the centre.

8. Working from point 4 and using the distance between point 4 and A, mark off the same distance around the circumference with a pair of compasses. This will give you a 4-sided shape.

9. Draw a circle using the distance between point 5 and A and repeat step 8 to produce a 5-sided shape – a pentagon.

Fig. 3.50
Constructing regular polygons

This method of construction allows you to draw any regular polygon. Simply follow steps 1 to 6 and mark off the required number of sides on the vertical line (e.g. mark off 6 points to draw a hexagon, 7 for a heptagon and 8 for an octagon). Try it for yourself. You will need to draw accurately with drawing instruments.

82

Constructing an ellipse

Ellipses are commonly used in logos and sign design. Both Land Rover and the Ford Motor Company use them in their designs. There are several ways of constructing an ellipse using geometry, but the auxiliary circle method shown here is probably the simplest.

Fig. 3.51 *The Land Rover logo*

1. Draw the axes AB and CD.

2. Draw the major circle and the minor circle on the axes.

3. Divide the circles into an equal number of parts by radial lines through point O.

4. Where the radial lines cut the major auxiliary circle, draw a perpendicular line. Where the radial lines cut the minor auxiliary circle, draw a horizontal line. The intersection of these two lines are points on the ellipse.

5. Use French curves or a flexi-curve to join up the points and complete the ellipse. Note that for clarity, only two points in each quadrant have been plotted in this example. In order to draw a more accurate curve, at least four points in each quadrant should be plotted.

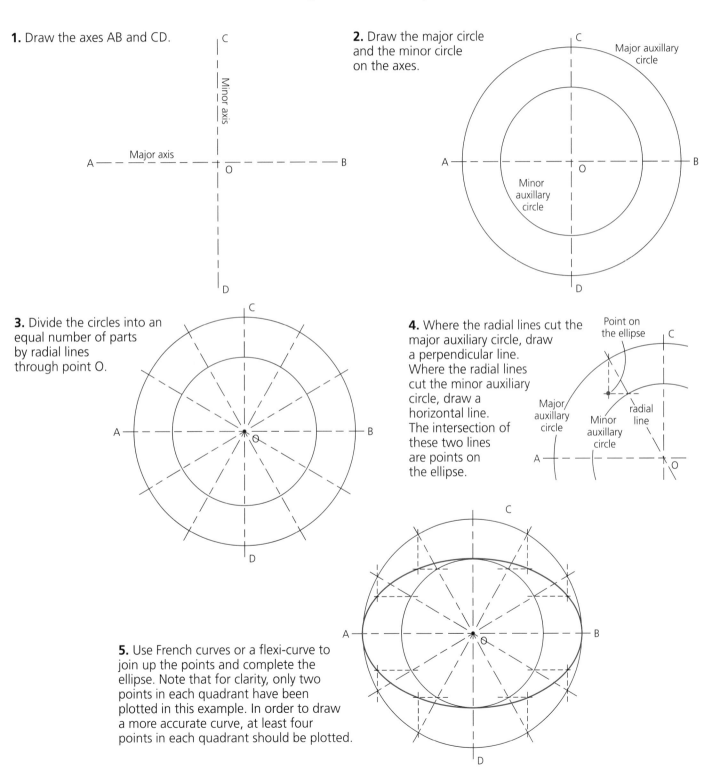

Fig. 3.52 *Constructing an ellipse using the auxiliary circle method*

Putting it into practice

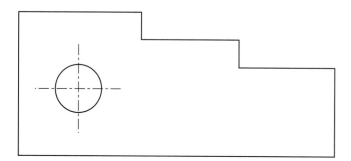

1 Copy the drawing shown above and then dimension it according to British standards.

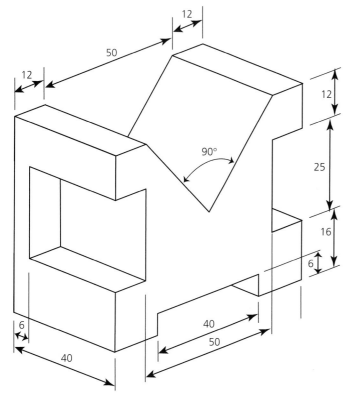

2 The drawing above shows an engineering tool called a vee block. Draw the vee block accurately using first angle orthographic projection.

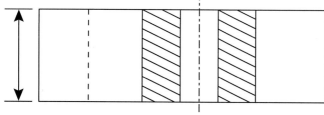

3 The drawing shown above consists of several different types of line. Identify each type and explain its uses.

4 Choose a simple object such as a matchbox, cassette or CD case and make a section drawing of it.

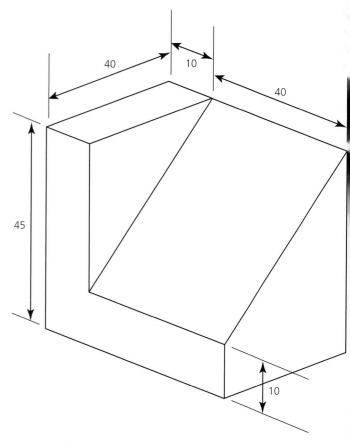

5 Make a third angle orthographic drawing of the block shown in the drawing above.

What do the following abbreviations stand for?

a) CL **b)** cm **c)** A/F

d) CRS **e)** DIA **f)** DRG

g) HEX HD **h)** I/D **i)** MTL

7 Explain the advantages of using ICT to produce technical drawings.

8 Draw a straight horizontal line, 75 mm, long and then bisect it.

9 Construct a regular hexagon with a side length of 45 mm.

10 Construct an ellipse with a major axis of 150 mm and a minor axis of 70 mm.

11 Draw a line 85 mm long and then, by construction, divide it into 6 equal parts,

12 Draw an angle of 60° and then bisect it.

13 Using only a pair of compasses, ruler and pencil, construct an equilateral triangle with a base of 75 mm.

14 Name four parts of a circle.

15 Design a logo using your initials and enclose it within a regular octagon.

84

4· Modelling and prototyping

Modelling allows designers to visualise their ideas as 3-dimensional objects. This helps them to test and develop their ideas further, before making the final product. Models are also a way of presenting final ideas that can be easily understood by everyone, not just the experts. It is easier to look at a model than to read complex working drawings.

Graphic designers produce mock-ups of page designs, brochures etc. to show their clients. Architects model building designs and photograph them to find out how it will affect the environment. Dummy products are modelled and evaluated to find out the views of potential customers. Modelling covers a range of activities, from working with paper and card to sophisticated computer models.

Fig. 4.2 *Architects discussing a model*

Fig. 4.1 *This exhibition stand would have started as a mock-up or model for the client.*

3-dimensional modelling is important in the designing process of your project work in school. Once you have generated your ideas, you will be expected to develop them using models. Modelling allows you to try out different ideas or concepts or test to see if mechanical devices and systems work.

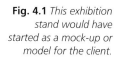

Models give you information about size and form and help you to determine if the parts of your product will fit together. Modelling can also help you to decide which materials are most suitable to use and try out assembly methods and procedures.

Prototype models

Prototype models are made during the manufacturing stage of a product, just before the production run begins. They are not models in the true sense of the word, because they do actually work and in some cases the prototype is the first product to be manufactured. They are created so that the 'real thing' can be tested and checked to ensure that it meets the needs identified in the specification, and any final design problems can be solved, before the product goes into full production. Computer technology allows designers to make very quick prototypes of their designs using rapid prototyping process.

Fig. 4.3 *Prototype model of a miniature television*

85

Alan Miller Bunford is a freelance stage designer and scenic artist. He designs and oversees the making of stage sets for plays, musicals and pantomimes for both regional and West End theatres.

*Once he has read his client's script and discussed the director's particular interpretations of the production, he sketches an outline ground plan giving a bird's eye view of the set. This will be drawn to **scale** and will give **dimensions** for the model to be constructed.*

Presentation models

Presentation models are used to show what a finished product will look like. Designers often refer to this kind of model as a '**mock-up**'. A variety of different materials and techniques can be used to achieve a realistic model, depending upon the nature and size of the finished product. In the car industry, full-size mock-ups of cars are made to find out what people think about the shape and style before the car goes into production. The model of the glue gun (Fig. 4.4) has been made so that its shape, style and ergonomic performance can be assessed. It may only be a model of a glue gun, but a high level of realism has been obtained by the skills of the model maker.

Fig. 4.5 *Example of a simple sketch model showing a mechanism*

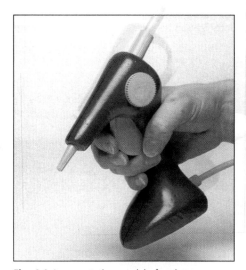

Fig. 4.4 *A presentation model of a glue gun*

Sketch models

Sketch models, like freehand sketches, are used to explore design concepts and to develop ideas. They are a quick way of giving an impression of size, shape and form. They allow the 3-dimensional development of ideas. Sketch models can also be used to experiment with mechanisms and working principles that may be needed in a design. This type of modelling is used by designers to visualise and clarify their ideas. The models are not normally meant to be presented to the client. Almost any suitable sheet material and fasteners can be used – stiff card, paper fasteners and a variety of everyday materials are frequently used to model mechanisms.

Demonstration models

Demonstration models are built to show other people how something works. They are very useful for demonstrating principle or method of operation. The model shown in Fig. 4.6 demonstrates how a solar heating system works.

Fig. 4.6 *A demonstration model of a solar heating system*

86

Some of his stage designs require extensive research, especially if the script is set in a particular architectural period. One project, a play called 'The Cemetery Club' involved investigating Jewish cemeteries in the Bronx (in New York) to ensure that the way the gravestones were represented was authentic.

The next step involves the construction of a scale 3D **model** made out of card and balsa wood. Miniature furniture and other objects will be included in preparation for a meeting with the director. In the photo on the right you can see the model of the revolving stage set that Alan made for a play called 'Holmes and the Ripper'.

Computer modelling

Information and communication technology is an important and very useful tool in the modelling process. Some CAD packages such as *ProDesktop* allow you to create 3-dimensional solid models on screen. These can be converted into working drawings, photographic quality rendered drawings or special data files which enable computer controlled machines to manufacture the design .

Virtual prototyping

The production of high quality computer generated models which can be printed out in photographic quality is sometimes referred to as virtual prototyping. They have a major advantage over traditional airbrush and marker renderings because any changes made to the design of the model are automatically made to the image when it is updated.

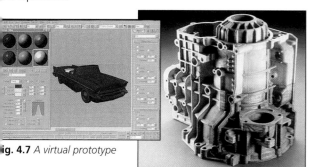

Fig. 4.7 *A virtual prototype*

Rapid prototyping

Rapid prototyping allows designers to build up a 3-dimensional image, from a computer model, in layers rather than by wasting or removing unwanted material. It provides designers with the opportunity to quickly build 3-dimensional models which they can show to clients, test or use as patterns for manufacture. Laser technology is used to produce prototypes from a range of materials including resin bonded paper, sintered plastics and metals, as well as polyester resin.

It is possible to carry out rapid prototyping in schools using a special software wizard and a *Roland Camm 1* cutter plotter. The software imports a solid model and 'slices' it into layers. The slices are then cut out of sticky-backed paper on the cutter. The slices are numbered and registration holes are cut so that the model can be assembled easily. Graphics can then be applied and the finished model used as a promotional product.

Fig. 4.8 *Rapid prototyping using resin bonded paper – Laminated Object Manufacture (LOM)*

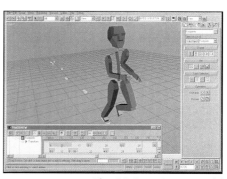

Fig. 4.9 *On-screen 3D model*

Computer simulation

Simulation is an aspect of modelling in which test conditions can be simulated by the computer. It is used in industry when it is too expensive or too dangerous to carry out real life testing. Many computer aided design software packages include animation and kinematic motion facilities which can be used to move designs on screen in order to test their function and investigate how parts of the product relate to each other.

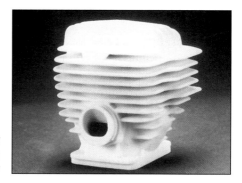

Fig. 4.10 *Rapid prototype model of a motorcycle cylinder*

Following the meeting with the director of the play, Alan Miller Bunford makes amendments to his stage-set model before preparing construction drawings from which the set will be built (you can see him preparing these drawings in the photo on the left). Detailed costings can be made at this point and he will maintain close contact with the builders throughout the set construction.

Most of the stage sets that Alan designs are for touring productions, so it is crucial that they are easy to dismantle and re-erect in a very short time. They must also be very robust in order to stand up to the constant moves.

Materials

Models can be made from a wide variety of materials, using many different methods and techniques. You can buy materials made especially for modelling from specialist suppliers, but many suitable modelling materials should be available in school. Many of the materials used for modelling will also be suitable for manufacturing your finished product. Take care to choose the most appropriate materials for the job and also consider how the product will be manufactured when choosing materials. Most Graphic Products projects will be manufactured from lightweight materials and will often need to be flat-packed. It is best to avoid making large structures from heavy materials such as wood and MDF. These materials can be used to support lightweight structures, but are best avoided as main modelling or construction materials in this subject.

Paper and card

Paper and card are among the most widely used materials for making models. They are relatively inexpensive and easy to work with, requiring simple tools and equipment. They are available in an enormous range of thicknesses, colours and surface finishes.

Plastic materials

Most plastic sheet materials are useful for model making. They allow construction in a similar way to card, but they are stronger, more hard-wearing and do not warp or distort in a damp atmosphere. Thermoplastic sheet (e.g. acrylic or polystyrene) can be heated and bent into shape. If you are not happy with the result, you can reheat it and bend it again. It is relatively easy to work with, requiring simple tools and equipment and very little finishing. 3-dimensional forms can be made from high impact polystyrene sheet by vacuum forming over a suitable former.

Fig. 4.11 *Modelling materials*

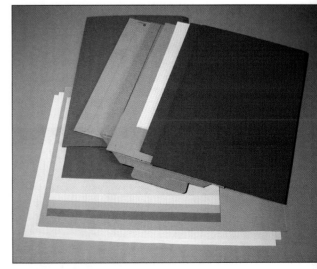

Fig. 4.12 *Paper and card*

Timber frames, covered in plywood or scenic canvas provide the background for the sets. He also uses fibreglass, expanded foam and sugar glass (for windows). All materials used, both in the construction and painting of the set, and the moveable objects (such as furniture) must be fire-retardant or non-combustible. Alan usually has a separate budget to provide furniture, floor covering and special props.

On occasions, Alan has also designed and cut out costumes for a production. For a play called 'The Red Barn' he produced 50 costumes, including the gentlemen's toppers. Making stage costumes is very different from making everyday garments – they are 'built', not tailored, and they need to be built to enable quick changes, with velcro for fastenings; false fronts to waistcoats and shirts, etc.

Alan's projects have included sets for a pop concert, Tupperware conference, Police Crime Prevention stand, and painted cloths for the Edinburgh Festival Theatre. The photo above shows a typical theatre set.

Foam board

Foam board is made from extruded foam polystyrene, sandwiched between thin layers of white ABS plastic. It is easily cut with a saw or a modelling knife and its smooth surface allows application of most paints and varnishes.

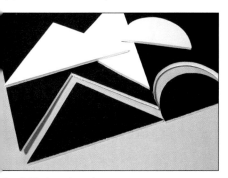

Fig. 4.13 Foam board

Rigid foam material

There are a number of rigid plastic foam materials for modelling. Styrofoam is probably the best known. Foams can be cut using saws or a hot wire cutter and shaped and sanded with normal hand tools. The denser types of foam can be machined on computer controlled milling machines or routers, allowing 3D computer models to be produced. Some foams are even dense enough to be used to make vacuum forming patterns or moulds.

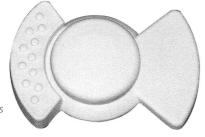

Fig. 4.14 Plastic foams

Plasticard

Plasticard is styrene sheet that can be cut with a small saw or sharp knife and joined using polystyrene cement. Liquid cement such as 'liquid poly' is the most effective, as it can be applied very accurately with a small brush. Plasticard is available in plain flat sheets and embossed sheets, which represent a variety of surfaces including bricks, tiles, paving slabs and timber.

Fig. 4.15 Plasticard sheets and adhesive

Corriflute

Corriflute is polypropylene sheet which is reinforced inside with flutes, rather like corrugated card. It is strong, light and colourful and can be easily cut with a modelling knife or saw.

Wood

A variety of natural wood and wood products can be used for modelling. Lightweight sheet material such as balsa and thin ply are most commonly used by model makers. Hardwood such as jelutong and manufactured board such as MDF (medium-density fibre board) are also suitable for supporting and strengthening lightweight structures. Take care that dusty materials such as MDF are only sanded in well-ventilated areas.

Metal

Metal in the form of strip and wire can be bent and shaped to form supports for less rigid modelling materials. Frames or armatures used for work with soft modelling materials such as clay, plasticine and papier-mâché can be made from wire and thin rod.

Fig. 4.16 Models made from Corriflute

SMART MATERIALS

New materials are constantly being developed as technology progresses and many of these can be used in graphic products. In packaging, for example, self-bonding corrugated card is now used. Thermal inks, which produce a raised surface when heated, have been used for some time. Many of the new materials that are now developed are **smart materials**. Smart materials respond to changes in temperature, light or voltage.

Thermocolour sheet

Thermocolour sheet is a liquid crystal ink impregnated self-adhesive film that changes colour as the temperature changes. As a flat sheet material, it lends itself to a wide range of graphic product applications. This technology has been used for many years in LCD displays in products such as laptop computers, calculators and watches, where it responds to electrical signals. Thermochromatic liquid crystals are turned into minute capsules which are then turned into an ink which can be printed onto plastic or paper. With the use of resistance wire, which heats up when an electrical current is passed through it, thermocolour sheet can be used to make advertising signs and displays. The sheet changes from black to blue at 27 °C, so only a low voltage is required.

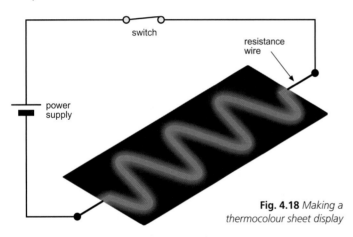

Fig. 4.18 *Making a thermocolour sheet display*

Lenticular sheet

Lenticular polypropylene sheet has a number of uses in Graphic Products. It gives the optical illusion that it is actually 6 mm thick instead of less than 1 mm. When placed on top of an object or image it makes it appear to sink below the surface. It can also be used to create 3D effects or simple animations. It has been used for displays, badges, postcards and record and CD sleeves for a number of years.

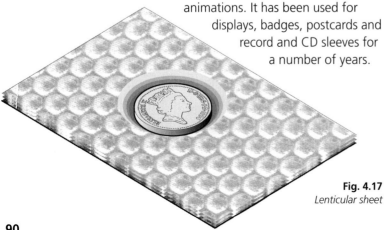

Fig. 4.17 *Lenticular sheet*

Polymorph

Polymorph is a tough plastic material which fuses and becomes easily mouldable at 62 °C. It can be heated in hot water or with a hairdryer and moulded by hand.

It can be used for a number of things including moulding handles, making vacuum forming moulds and prototyping mechanical parts. Polymorph is non-hazardous, biodegradable and very strong and tough. It can be moulded between 62 °C and 30 °C. Care needs to be taken when moulding. After removing the material from boiling water, allow it to cool slightly before moulding in your hands.

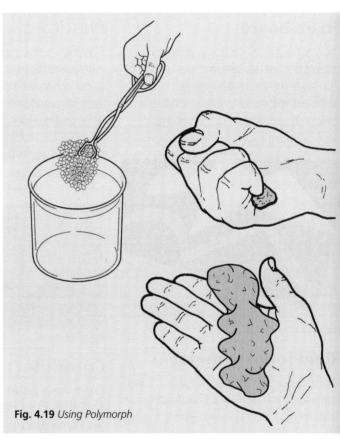

Fig. 4.19 *Using Polymorph*

Smart wire

Smart wire is a form of **shape memory alloy (SMA)**, a mixture of nickel and titanium, called nitinol. It can be made to remember a shape as a result of heat treatment. If bent at room temperature into a paper clip shape, it will stay bent, but if the temperature is raised above 70 °C, it will straighten out. The temperature can be raised by passing a current through it, so it can therefore be used to provide movement or control in Graphic Products projects

MODELLING TOOLS

In addition to the usual range of workshop tools such as files, saws and drills, there are some specialist modelling tools that will be useful to you.

Scalpel
For accurate cutting of thin sheet material.

Craft knife
For cutting heavier materials.

Cutting mat
To protect the work surface and prolong the life of the blades. All cutting should be done on a cutting mat.

A compass cutter
A compass cutter is used for cutting circles and ellipses in card.

Safety ruler
A safety ruler with a raised edge to protect your fingers should always be used when using a craft knife or scalpel.

A rotary cutter
Rotary cutters are an alternative to craft knives for cutting straight lines in card.

A perforating tool
This is used to cut a series of tiny holes in card but if used carefully it can score card prior to bending.

Fig. 4.20 *Specialist modelling tools from the olfa range*

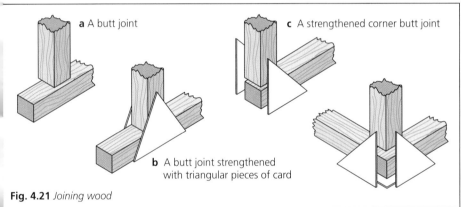

a A butt joint

c A strengthened corner butt joint

b A butt joint strengthened with triangular pieces of card

Fig. 4.21 *Joining wood*

Fig. 4.22 *Using card*

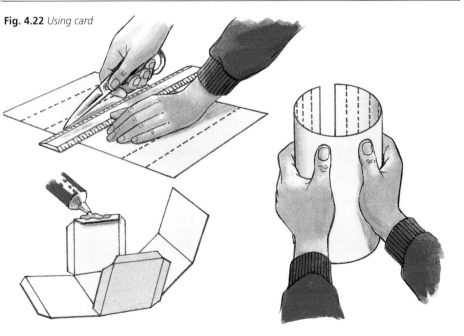

Fabricating models

Fabricating is when models are made by joining materials or parts together. They are joined **temporarily**, using joints such as paper fasteners or Velcro, which can both be taken apart, or **permanently**, using glue.

Almost any sheet material can be used for fabricating models. Balsa wood, thin plywood and plastic sheet, but paper and card are probably the most widely used materials. Card should be scored before folding to allow neat crisp edges to be formed. This can be done by running either the tip of a pair of scissors or a special scoring tool (Fig. 4.22) along the line of the bend before folding. Curved surfaces can be formed by scoring a series of lines and gently curving the card to the shape required. Fabricated models can be reinforced using a framework of thin strips of balsa. The frame can be joined together using card triangles (Fig. 4.21).

The best way of making card models is to form them from a development with tabs added to enable the model to be securely fixed (developments are explained in detail over the page).

Tony Childs and Eddie Arnold are designers at LINPAC, a company that designs and makes packaging. Almost every type of product – from cosmetics to horticultural produce – requires some form of packaging.

*The designers often use a basic **development** as a starting point, and then make adaptations according to customers' requirements. The photograph here shows a development on screen of a 'carry-home pack' for dot matrix printers. While working on a project, the designers ensure*

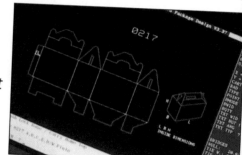

optimum 'palletisation' – in other words, they make sure that the design fits together well and the maximum number of packages will fit on to a pallet. The CAD package the designers use will also take into account the weight of the product and how high the packages will be stacked in order to calculate the strength of the material needed.

DEVELOPMENTS

A **development** is a drawing that shows an object as if all its surfaces had been opened out on to one plane. Developments are often used as patterns or templates when working in sheet materials because they show the true shape of the object. Fig. 4.23 and Fig. 4.24 show a third angle orthographic drawing of a dice and its development. To understand it easily, imagine a cube made of card that has been unfolded. This unfolded shape is known as the development.

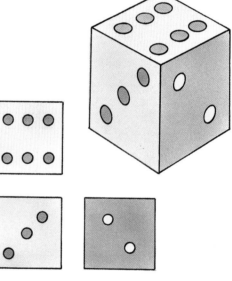

Fig. 4.23

Tabs can easily be added to developments so that they can be cut out and assembled. Tabs can then be stuck down using double sided tape to complete the model.

Developments can be drawn using computer software such as *Techsoft 2D Designer* and cut out using a *Roland Camm 1 cutter*.

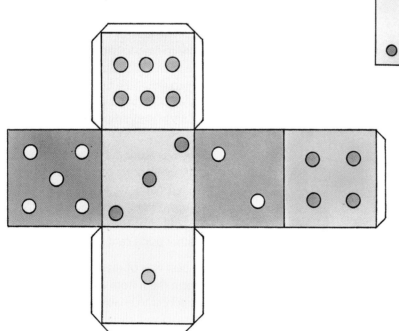

Fig. 4.24 *The development of the cube with tabs*

LINPAC supplies all sorts of packaging. As well as cardboard boxes their range includes expanded polystyrene foam packs, paper sacks, plastic films, and metal closures and cans. They also design and provide customised artwork for printing. The photograph shown here includes some examples of the finished cardboard developments that LINPAC supply to their customers.

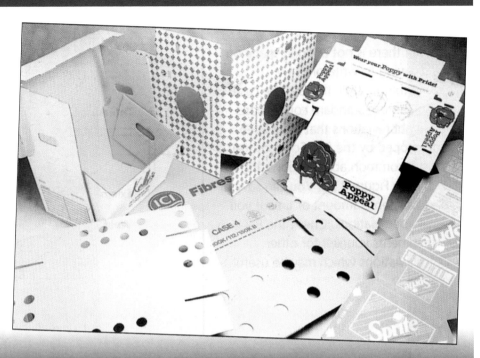

Developments of curved surfaces

Drawing developments of objects with curved surfaces requires the use of some simple geometry. To draw the development of a cylinder like the one shown in Fig. 4.25, you need to draw an accurate front elevation and plan first. The height of the development will be the height of the front elevation. One way to find the width is to divide the plan into 12 equal 30° segments by measuring one and stepping off the rest with compasses or dividers. Now draw these segments as if they were flattened out – you will have drawn a rectangle, which is the true shape of the curved surface. Another way of finding the width of the development is to calculate mathematically the circumference of the plan.

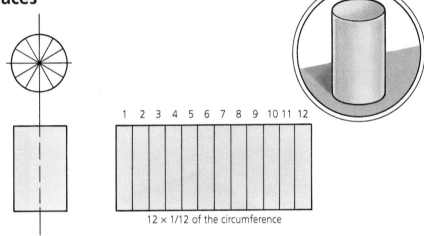

12 × 1/12 of the circumference

Fig. 4.25 *Stages in drawing the development of a cylinder*

The development of a cone is a sector of a circle (Fig. 4.26). It is drawn using the same principle. The true length of the cone's side (the slant height) provides the two straight edges of the development.

To calculate how big a sector the development needs to be, measure the distance across one 30° sector on the plan and step it off on the development 12 times.

The truncated cone in Fig. 4.27 would be developed in a similar way, except that two concentric circles would have to be drawn. Try drawing a development of it yourself.

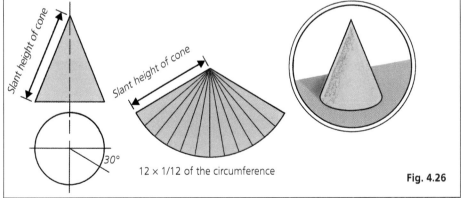

Slant height of cone

Slant height of cone

30°

12 × 1/12 of the circumference

Fig. 4.26   **Fig. 4.27**

FORMING

Thermoplastics are easy to form. When they are softened by heating, they become very pliable. Strips of acrylic for example, can even be tied in knots, like a ribbon, when they are hot. Remember that you must wear protective gloves when trying this. Thermosetting plastics, due to their physical properties, cannot be heated and formed in this way. Once formed, they cannot be heated and re-shaped.

Line bending

You may need to bend plastic sheet material in straight lines, in the same way as you bend card. If you heat a whole sheet it is very difficult to bend the material accurately. The easiest way is to use a line bender which only heats the area that needs bending (Fig. 4.30). To do this, hold the acrylic over the strip heater and when the plastic is soft, bend it gently. It is best if you can use a former to achieve the correct angle of bend (Fig. 4.29). This also allows you to hold the plastic steady whilst it is cooling and stiffening. Some strip heaters have a guide to hold the material in place while it cools.
This can be preset to the required angle.

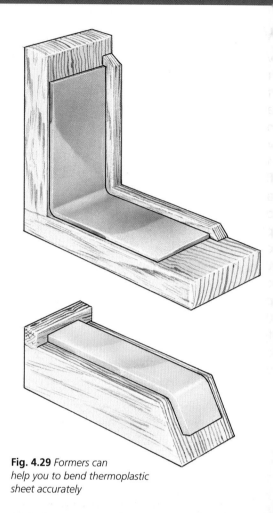

Fig. 4.29 Formers can help you to bend thermoplastic sheet accurately

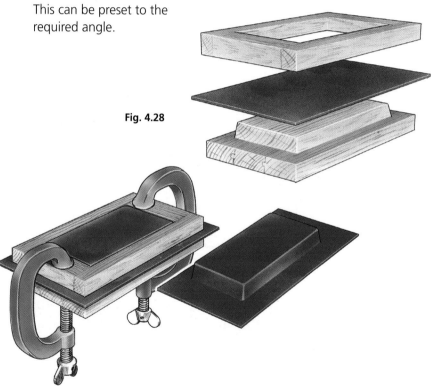

Fig. 4.28

Press forming

Acrylic can be press formed easily when heated. The temperature that is required to soften acrylic is around 160 °C. This can be achieved by using an oven set at the correct temperature (**remember to wear protective gloves**). Acrylic cools slowly, because it is a poor conductor of heat. It assumes the shape that it has been formed in when hot. Pressing the acrylic into a mould when soft can produce many different shapes. Dishes and containers can be made very easily. A two-part former can be used to mould the acrylic (Fig. 4.28). The mould must not be opened, however, until the acrylic is cool or it will not freeze into the new shape. The moulded acrylic can then be trimmed, if required.

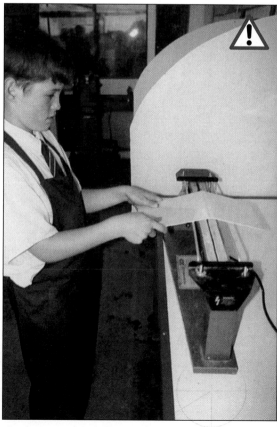

Fig. 4.30 Using a strip heater for line bending

Vacuum forming

Vacuum forming in industry can be found in the Industrial Perspectives section earlier in this book. Vacuum forming is a useful and effective way of forming plastics for model making and for project work. The vacuum forming process works by removing air from underneath the soft and flexible thermoplastic sheet, allowing atmospheric pressure to push the plastic down on to a mould (Fig. 4.32). Various packaging items with complex deep shapes can be formed using this process, including trays, dishes and masks. Most of the common thermoplastics are suitable – polythene, PVC, high-impact polystyrene (HIP), ABS and acrylic. There are different types of vacuum forming machines which affect the size, capacity and shape of the work. A typical school machine is shown in Fig. 4.31.

Fig. 4.31 *A school vacuum forming machine*

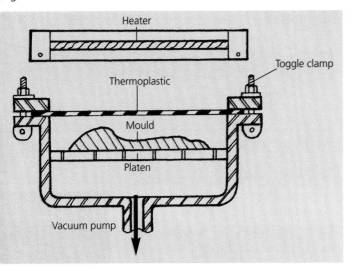

Fig. 4.32 *Vacuum forming*

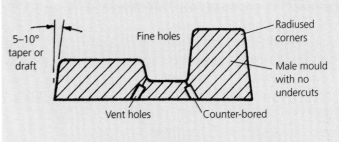

Fig. 4.33 *Mould design*

The quality of the mould design will determine the result. Moulds require slight tapering, usually between 5° to 10° with any sharp corners rounded, to allow the formed shape to be easily removed. The material from which the mould is made must withstand heat and slight pressure, and have smooth mark-free surfaces to avoid showing faults on the finished moulding. Moulds may also require 'venting' (Fig. 4.33) to ensure that all the air between the mould and the material is evacuated as quickly as possible. Venting involves drilling small diameter holes, counter-bored from the underside, in awkward positions (i.e. depressions and cavities) where air might become trapped.

Thermoplastic sheet is clamped firmly in place, forming an airtight seal. Radiant heat is applied from a moveable element above the plastic sheet. When plasticity is achieved, air is evacuated from the chamber by means of a vacuum pump. The resulting air pressure above the sheet forces it tightly around the mould, which rests on the platen. Deep moulds can cause problems, such as thinning on the side surfaces, as the plastic is drawn down.

Fig. 4.34 *This mask was produced by vacuum forming*

95

MOULDING

Creating block models by moulding pliable materials is a useful way of producing static models of dummy products. The traditional materials of clay, papier-mâché, plaster and plasticine have largely been replaced by more modern materials. Car manufacturers, however, still make full-size clay models of their designs. These materials are often still available in school and can be used to produce realistic models.

Clay, plasticine and papier-mâché

The best way to construct models made from clay, plasticine or papier-mâché is to build them over a framework structure (known as an 'armature'). The skeleton frame is usually built on a baseboard of wood and then covered with wire mesh or perforated aluminium sheet to support the modelling material. Using an armature reduces the amount of modelling material required and so reduces the weight and cost of the finished model.

Fig. 4.35

Air-drying modelling clays

A number of air-drying modelling materials, such as Das Pronto, Newclay and Mod-Roc, are now available and because they do not need to be fired in a kiln to harden them, they are very easy and convenient to use.

Fig. 4.36

Das Pronto is a specially formulated air hardening material, it is exceptionally soft and pliable and is easy to use. It will produce long lasting models providing a clay type finish that can be decorated with paints and then varnished. Unused material must be kept in a plastic bag to prevent it from hardening. Newclay is a very similar material but a special hardener can be used with it to increase its durability. Mod-Roc is a fine gauze material that is impregnated with quick drying plaster which means it can be bandaged to virtually any surface. Basic structures can be built using cardboard, polystyrene, wire mesh etc. and covered with Mod-Roc.

Polymer clays

These materials are not technically clays at all, but a plastic material with working properties that resemble clay. *Fimo* and *Formello* are commonly used brands of polymer clay and are available in a wide range of colours. They can be kept separate, to avoid the need to paint the model, or intermixed, to achieve subtle blends or a marbled effect. Polymer clays stay soft and pliable until baked to permanent hardness in an oven. They are hardened by heating to 130 °C in a conventional home oven for between 15 to 20 minutes. Once cool they are permanently hard and can be painted or varnished if required. Take care when using ovens. Wear oven gloves to remove models. **Never put polymer clays into a microwave oven**. They were not designed to be hardened in this way and it can be very dangerous.

Fig. 4.37

96

Wasting

The process of creating a shape by removing material is known as wasting. This can be done using hand tools such as saws, planes and files, or it can be done using computer controlled milling machines or routers. Block models can be produced in this way from plastic foams, balsa wood and hard wax.

Styrofoam

Styrofoam is a high-density expanded polystyrene foam that is clean and safe to use. The easiest way to cut it is to use a hot wire cutter, but you can also use a hand saw, vibrating saw or bandsaw. Styrofoam does not generate dust or toxic fumes when being cut and is easy to sand with fine glass paper or 'wet and dry'. To give it a suitable surface for painting, cover the Styrofoam with a thin layer of a solution made from plaster, PVA adhesive and water. Allow it to dry and then sand the surface. Remember to take care when sanding plastic materials such as Styrofoam – always work in a well ventilated area and avoid inhaling dust and fumes.

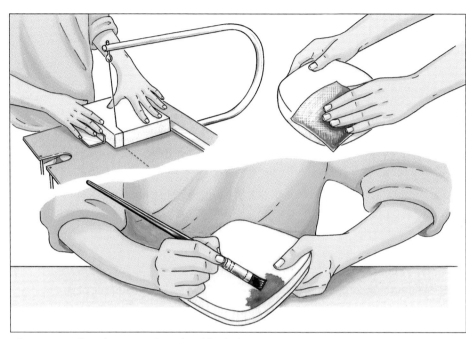

Fig. 4.38 *Styrofoam being cut, shaped and finished*

Using CADCAM

3D solid models designed on computer can be made by exporting the STL file (Stereolithography file) directly to the computer controlled machine. Some of the earlier machines may require you to use a machining wizard such as *MiniCAM* to convert the model to a file that can be read by the machine. The finished design can be machined in modelling foam or modelling wax.

Modelling foam

A special closed cell rigid plastic foam can be used for modelling and can be machined at high speed with very little tool wear. There are two types of foam available, **low density**, which allows rough models to be made at low cost, and **high density**, which has greater structural strength and gives better surface detail, making it ideal for finished models. After painting or varnishing, the high density foam can be vacuum formed over.

Fig. 4.39 *Machining a computer generated model*

Modelling wax

This is a hard wax formulated specifically for machining on computer controlled milling machines. It allows products to be machined at high feeds and speeds to give the shortest possible machining time. It is ideal for vacuum forming over, and although initially expensive to buy, it may be melted down and reused.

MODELLING WITH KITS

Modelling kits are very effective for communicating mechanical ideas. The advantages of kits over other materials are that they can be assembled quickly, dismantled after use, and used again and again. *Lego*, *Fischer Technik* and *Meccano* kits are the more popular kits that are used for this purpose. Meccano is perhaps the most versatile, but it does take longer to assemble as it requires the use of nuts and bolts. Modelling kits are not normally used for presentation models, but they are widely used for sketch modelling, especially when mechanical systems are involved.

Modelling accessories

Models can be made to show a great deal of detail and look very realistic by using specialist modelling accessories. There is a wide range of architectural and interior design components available from model-making suppliers. These include scale figures, household fittings, trees, fences and cars.

Gears, motors, wheels and other details used in demonstration modelling are difficult and time-consuming to make from scratch, so these can also be bought from model-making suppliers.

Fig. 4.40 *Modelling accessories, gears and motors*

Components

A whole range of components can be used for joining and fixing models: nails, screws, nuts and bolts etc.

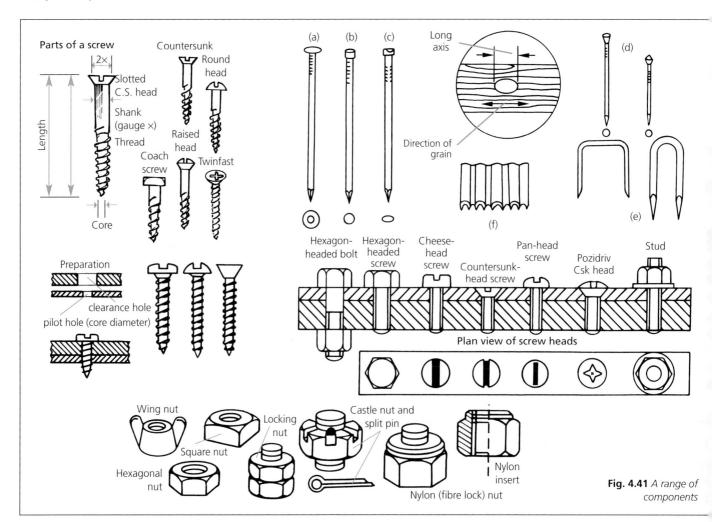

Fig. 4.41 *A range of components*

98

ADHESIVES

There are a number of adhesives that can be used for bonding materials in graphic products. It is important to select the most suitable adhesive for the materials you want to bond together. The chart in Fig. 4.43 will help you to decide what to use. In addition to the adhesives available, double sided tape, hot melt glue guns and glue sticks such as *Pritt Stik* all have their place in joining materials. Always follow the instructions carefully and remember that many adhesives can be harmful.

Fig. 4.42 *Hot melt glue gun*

Metal	Contact adhesive	Double side tape	Epoxy resin	Contact adhesive		Epoxy resin
MDF	PVA		Contact adhesive	PVA		Epoxy resin
Wood	PVA		Contact adhesive	PVA		Epoxy resin
Balsa	Contact adhesive	PVA	Contact adhesive	Balsa cement	PVA	Epoxy resin
Acrylic	Contact adhesive	Double side tape	Contact adhesive	Tensol No. 12	Contact adhesive	Epoxy resin
Polystyrene sheet	Contact adhesive	Double side tape	Polystyrene cement	Contact adhesive		Epoxy resin
Rigid foam styrofoam	PVA	Double side tape		PVA		Double side tape
Foamboard	Contact adhesive	PVA	Contact adhesive			
Card	Contact adhesive	PVA	Contact adhesive			
Paper	Contact adhesive	PVA	Contact adhesive			
Fabric	Latex adhesive / Contact adhesive	PVA	Contact adhesive			

Fabric   Paper   Card   Foamboard   **Rigid foam styrofoam**   **Polystyrene sheet**   Acrylic   Balsa   Wood   MDF   Metal

Fig. 4.43 *Adhesive selection chart*

Read instructions for adhesives carefully

Finishing models

The final finishing of models is very important if a professional appearance is to be achieved. Epoxy resin fillers such as Plastic Padding or Isopon can be used to fill gaps and holes. This can be sanded with abrasive paper and painted with a primer. Primer fillers used in car body repairs can be sprayed on as several thin layers to gradually build up a good surface finish. Take care with fillers and spray paints, always read the instructions carefully and wear appropriate protective clothing.

Car body paint can be used to create an excellent surface finish, but care must be taken when using it. Acrylic paints also give good results and are safer to use.

Most models will need to be sealed to protect them. Card models can be painted with a thin coat of PVA before the final finishing.

Fig. 4.44 *Fillers and paints*

Fig. 4.45 *The Roland Stika machine*

Models can be given the finishing touch by applying graphics or lettering. Dry transfer lettering such as *Letraset* can be used or you can create your own using computer graphics software. Your own designs can be made using *Techsoft 2D Designer* and then cut out in self-adhesive vinyl sheet with a *Roland Camm1 cutter* or the smaller *Stikka* machine.

Putting it into practice

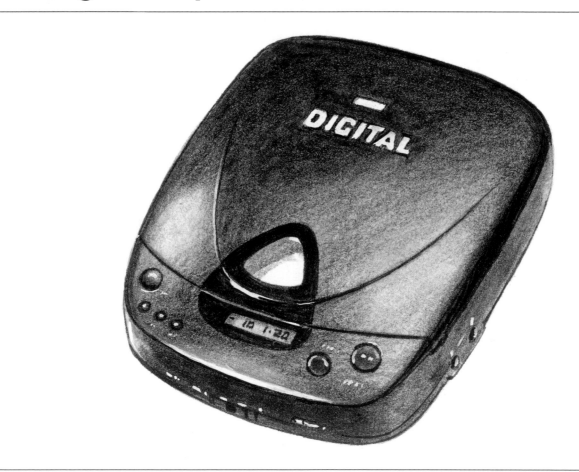

1 Explain what is meant by the term *smart material*.

2 Name a smart material used in graphic products and give an example of its use.

3 Name suitable adhesives for bonding the following material together:

   a) acrylic to acrylic,

   b) acrylic to high impact polystyrene sheet,

   c) styrofoam to styrofoam,

   d) styrofoam to acrylic,

   e) aluminium sheet to acrylic.

4 Name a suitable material for making a counter-top leaflet dispenser for a shop.

5 Suggest a suitable material to make a presentation model of a torch design.

6 Using a block of styrofoam or balsa wood, make a presentation model of the CD player shown above.

7 Using thin card, design and make a package for the CD player. Use clear acetate sheet to make a window so that the product can be seen.

8 Using vacuum formed, clear polystyrene sheet and card, make a model of a package for a small product such as a toy car, pencils or a pencil sharpener.

9 Design and model a collecting box for a local charity. It must fold flat when not in use, but be strong enough to hold coins.

10 List the advantages of using air drying modelling clay and polymer clays instead of traditional clay.

5 · Systems and control

Systems, in Design and Technology, provide us with a way of looking at things. They help us to understand how things work and enable us to make design decisions. A system consists of a group of parts or components which work together to make something happen. Systems have three parts: an **input**, a **process** and an **output**. They can be easily understood by using a box diagram like the one in Fig. 5.1. Rotary paper trimmers, although simple, are examples of systems. The input is the effort of sliding the cutter, the process is the cutting action of the trimmer and the output is the cut paper. The computer printer is also a good example of a system. Digital data, ink and paper are used to produce a printed page. Data from the computer, paper and ink are the input, the action of the print head is the process and the printed page is the output.

Fig. 5.2

INPUT	PROCESS	OUTPUT
Turning the key	The catch moves, unlocking the door	The door can be opened

Fig. 5.1 *A system block diagram*

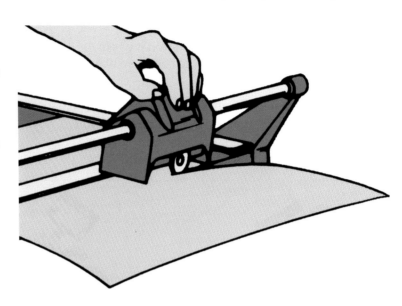

Feedback

The printer is a system which requires control. The page printed may not be of acceptable quality, it may be too light or too dark. In the printer control panel of the software, the function of the printer can be altered or controlled until it is of good enough quality. This form of control is known as feedback and the printer is a system with a **feedback** control loop. This is shown in the block diagram in Fig. 5.3.

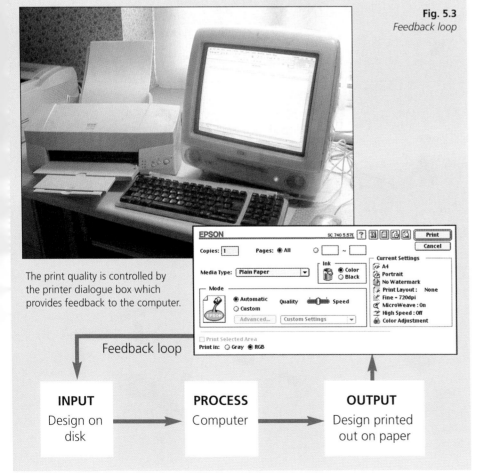

Fig. 5.3 *Feedback loop*

The print quality is controlled by the printer dialogue box which provides feedback to the computer.

Feedback loop

INPUT	PROCESS	OUTPUT
Design on disk	Computer	Design printed out on paper

Sub-systems

More complex systems consist of several sub-systems. These can be mechanical or electronic. The printer has mechanical systems which move the print head across the page and feed the paper into the machine. It also has an electronic system which converts the screen image into spots of ink which are sprayed onto the paper. In this section we will look at mechanical and electronic systems which may be used in Graphic Products.

Planning and control

Systems or a systems approach is also used to plan work in industry. Each stage of the design and manufacturing process is identified and decisions are made about when and how they will be carried out. Materials can be ordered and specific tasks planned to enable the products to be produced by the required deadline. This system can also be used when planning your project work in Graphic Products.

101

MECHANICAL SYSTEMS

Motion

When an object moves it is in motion. There are four types of motion used in mechanical systems. The type of motion is described by the way the object moves. **Rotary motion** is where the object follows a circular path around a central point, like a wheel or the hands of a clock. **Oscillating motion** is where the object swings from side to side like the pendulum of a clock or a child's swing.

Linear motion is movement in a straight line like that of a drawer or a paper trimmer. **Reciprocating motion** is backwards and forwards or up and down movement in a straight line, like that of a sewing machine needle.

Fig. 5.4 Four types of motion

Transferring motion

Mechanical systems transfer motion from one type to another or from one direction to another. The spiral ratchet screwdriver in Fig. 5.5 changes linear motion into rotary motion and the hand whisk transfers rotary motion through 90°.

Fig. 5.5 Transferring motion

Mechanical advantage

Mechanisms are designed to make things easier for us, so that we gain some advantage from them. This advantage is referred to as mechanical advantage.

Levers

The lever was one of the earliest mechanisms to be used and was probably first used during the Stone Age to move heavy boulders. It consists of a rigid bar with a fixed point called a **fulcrum** on which it turns. The lever is a system: the input is the effort applied and the output is the movement of the load. The mechanical advantage is gained by applying the effort at the end of the bar. More movement is needed here but much less effort is required. Scissors, shears, bottle openers and wheelbarrows are all examples of levers.

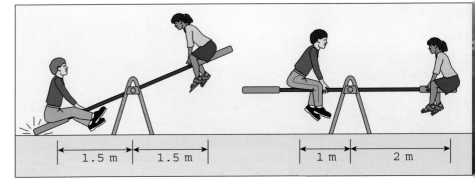

Fig. 5.6 Levers

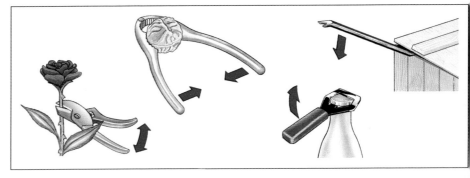

Fig. 5.7 Levers in everyday use

102

Linkages

Levers can be connected together to form linkages. They are used to link parts of a mechanical system together and can change the direction of forces. The linkage shown in Fig. 5.8 is used to reverse the direction of a force or movement. A pushing input motion is changed to a pulling output motion. The bell crank shown in Fig. 5.9 is used to transfer a force through 90°.

Linkages are also used to gain mechanical advantage in the same way as a lever. A small input force produces a larger output force because the pivot point is not in the middle of the link. This is shown in Fig. 5.10.

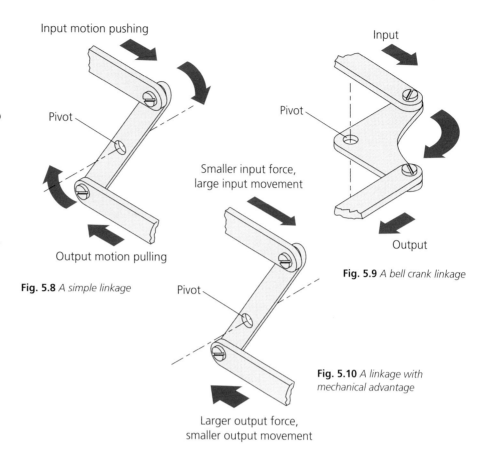

Input motion pushing

Pivot

Output motion pulling

Fig. 5.8 *A simple linkage*

Smaller input force, large input movement

Pivot

Input

Pivot

Output

Fig. 5.9 *A bell crank linkage*

Fig. 5.10 *A linkage with mechanical advantage*

Larger output force, smaller output movement

Cams

Cams are used to convert rotary motion to reciprocating motion. They are used in car engines to open valves, contact breakers and drive fuel pumps. Many different types of cams exist but the most useful for graphic products are rotary cams like the ones shown in Fig. 5.11. They can be pear-shaped or heart-shaped or round with an off-centre axle. This type is known as an **eccentric cam**.

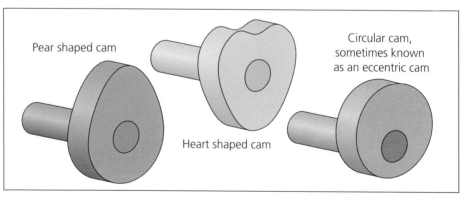

Pear shaped cam

Heart shaped cam

Circular cam, sometimes known as an eccentric cam

Fig. 5.11

Gears

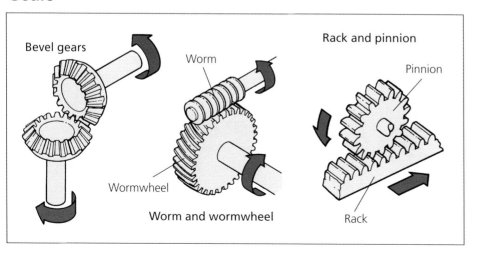

Bevel gears

Worm

Rack and pinnion

Pinnion

Wormwheel

Worm and wormwheel

Rack

Fig. 5.12

Gears are also used to change or transfer motion. They can be used to change the speed and the direction of rotary motion. They can be useful in Graphic Products for designing and making products such as rotating display stands or shop window displays. Plastic gears are available for use in project work in a number of different types and sizes from technology equipment suppliers.

USING MECHANISMS IN GRAPHIC PRODUCTS

Mechanisms can be used in a number of graphic products, ranging from moving toys to greetings cards, fold-flat advertising and pop-up books .
Fig. 5.13 shows how levers can be used to make simple card mechanisms. When using thin materials, the pivots can be made from paper fasteners, but when using thicker material, such as foamboard or corriflute, you may have to use nuts and bolts.

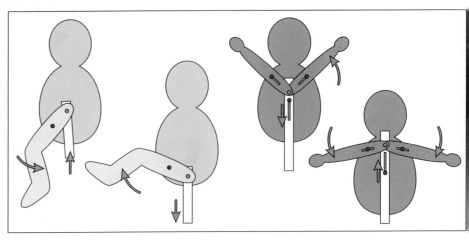

Fig. 5.13

Fold-flat advertising

This is an area of Graphic Products that uses simple mechanisms to make a variety of products that can be folded, put into envelopes and sent through the post. They are used by companies to advertise their products or services and can take the form of calendars, desk tidies and other office accessories.

Fig. 5.14

Holes for rubber band

Glue tabs

The one shown in Fig. 5.15 has been designed as a pencil holder and can display advertising graphics or data about a particular company. It is based on a regular hexagon with a trapezium attached to each side. The two shapes are glued together after having a rubber band stretched between two of the glue tabs. When the box is pressed flat the rubber band is stretched and when the shape is released the rubber band returns to its original length and pulls the box into shape (Fig. 5.16).

Rubber band pulls box into shape

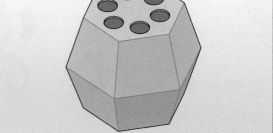

Fig. 5.15

Fig. 5.16

104

Pop-ups

Pop-up books and cards have been popular for many years and there are many different types on the market today. The first pop-up books were produced in the nineteenth century in England and then developed by German designers and publishers. Pop-ups are often aimed at the younger age group with their main advantage being that they bring books to life. Fig. 5.17 shows how pop-ups create a 3-dimensional effect and bring pages to life.

Pop-ups use a number of different mechanisms, some of which are very complicated. The ones shown here are simple examples which can easily be used in project work. You may be able to design your own.

Fig. 5.17

Multiple layers

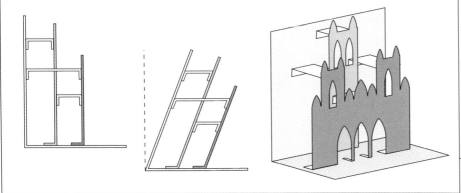

Fig. 5.18

The simplest pop-up mechanism is the multiple layer. This is based on a parallelogram and the pop-up uses one of the pages as its base. All the parts are parallel to each other, allowing them to fold flat when the book or card is closed.

Floating layers

Floating layers are similar to multiple layers except the layers are supported by pieces of card which lift it away from the page. This gives an impression of depth, especially when two or three layers are used on top of each other.

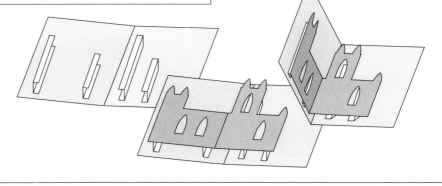

Fig. 5.19

The V fold

This is another useful pop-up mechanism which can be adapted to surprise the viewer when they open the book or card.

Levers, linkages and cams can be incorporated into the design of pop-ups with some very interesting effects.

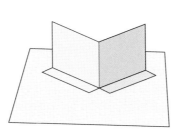

Fig. 5.20

105

ELECTRONIC SYSTEMS

Electronic systems are used to control many of the appliances we use in our homes. Although powered by electricity, washing machines, microwave ovens, CD players and central heating systems are all controlled by electronic circuits which use only a very small current. Electronic systems are used in graphic products to add interest and attract peoples attention. Musical greetings cards which play simple tunes using an integrated circuit, and badges with flashing lights are all commonly available graphic products.

Fig. 5.21 *Electronic systems used in graphic products*

Simple circuits

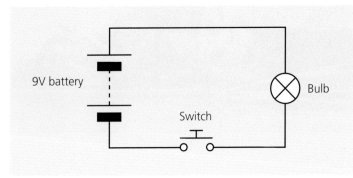

Fig. 5.22

Many electronic systems used in graphic products are very simple circuits which use only one or two components. Fig. 5.22 shows a circuit which uses a battery, a bulb and a switch. The circuit diagram is shown as a simple drawing using standard symbols for each component. Pressing the switch provides the input for this simple system, the supply of electricity is the process and the output is the bulb lighting. This circuit can be easily developed for use in graphic products by using a light emitting diode or LED. These are devices which glow when electricity is passed through them. They only allow electricity to flow in one direction and must therefore be correctly fitted into the circuit. LEDs are available in a number of colours and some flash automatically without the need for a control circuit.

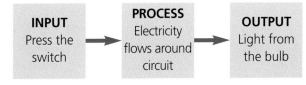

Fig. 5.23 *The system block diagram for the circuit above*

Modelling circuits

Circuit designs can be modelled and tested using computer aided design (CAD). *Crocodile Technology* is a very useful software package for electronic modelling. Circuits can be built on screen either graphically or using standard electronic symbols and then tested to see if they work. Your completed circuit design can then be used with other software to print out the design for the circuit board or PCB as it is known. If you do not have access to this software you will have to model your circuit using components and a modelling board.

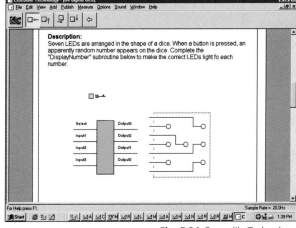

Fig. 5.24 *Crocodile Technology*

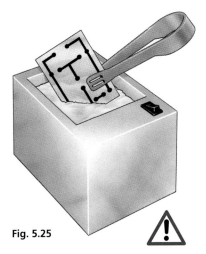

Fig. 5.25

Making the circuit board

When you have your finished circuit board design, it can be manufactured by either removing the unwanted copper from the board, using a computer controlled milling or engraving machine, or it can be etched, using ferric chloride. When working with card and paper you may not want to use a circuit board. Circuits can be made using self-adhesive copper strip. This is stuck directly onto the card and the components are then soldered to it. This is particularly useful when working on thin objects such as greetings cards or pop-up book pages.

Fig. 5.26 *Making a circuit using self-adhesive copper strip*

106

BASIC ELECTRONIC COMPONENTS

Switches

Switches are included in circuits to 'make ' or 'break' connections.

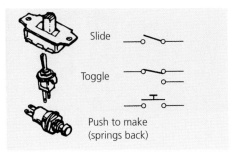

Fig 5.27

Resistors

Resistors resist and direct the flow of electricity. There are two basic types: **fixed** and **variable**. Fixed resistors have a fixed resistance which is indicated by a colour code. Resistance is measured in ohms, the symbol for which is W. The resistor colour codes are shown in Fig 5.33.

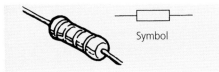

Fig 5.28 *A fixed resistor*

The resistance of a variable resistor can be changed by turning its spindle. You can set the resistance from zero up to the value given on the base of the component (e.g. 10kW).

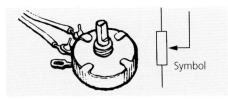

Fig 5.29 *A variable resistor*

A preset is a very small variable resistor. It can be adjusted using a small screwdriver.

Fig 5.30 *A preset resistor*

Sensors

A light dependent resistor (LDR) senses light and changes its resistance as the light intensity changes. Its resistance is *high* in the *dark* and *low* in the *bright light*.

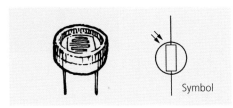

Fig 5.31

A thermistor senses heat and reacts to temperature changes. It has a *high* resistance when it is *cold*, and a *low* resistance when it is *hot*.

Fig 5.32 *Temperature sensor*

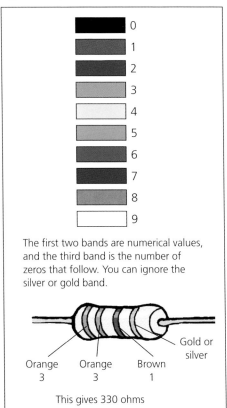

■	0
■	1
■	2
■	3
■	4
■	5
■	6
■	7
■	8
■	9

The first two bands are numerical values, and the third band is the number of zeros that follow. You can ignore the silver or gold band.

Orange 3   Orange 3   Brown 1   Gold or silver

This gives 330 ohms

Fig 5.33 *Resistor colour codes*

Output devices (transducers)

Bulbs can be connected either way round.

Fig 5.34 *Bulb*

LEDs (Light emitting diodes) are red, green or amber in colour. They must be connected the right way round and they need a protective resistor.

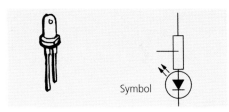

Fig 5.35 *Light emitting diode*

Buzzers give a continuous sound and make useful alarms.

Fig 5.36 *Buzzer*

Speakers can be used to create continuous noises, notes or speach.

Fig 5.37 *Speaker*

Small DC **motors** can be connected either way round, so running in either direction. They are used to create movement (e.g. in a model car).

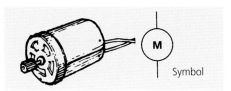

Fig 5.38 *Motor*

PLANNING AND CONTROL

Systems are used to plan and control work in industry. Planning is essential if the work is going to be carried out on time. After the client or customer has placed an order for a product, a production meeting takes place. At this meeting each stage of the project is identified and a sequence of operations or tasks is worked out. The required materials need to be ordered and artwork commissioned. Any specialist work which has to be carried out by outside agencies or contractors needs to be booked in. This type of detailed planning can be carried out using a flow chart.

Fig. 5.39 *A production meeting*

Flow charts

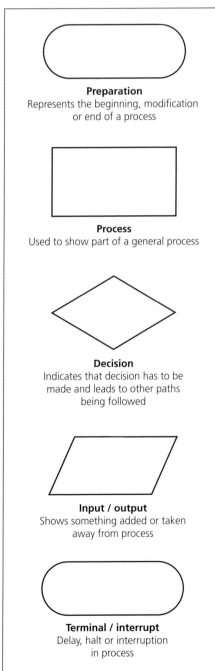

Preparation
Represents the beginning, modification or end of a process

Process
Used to show part of a general process

Decision
Indicates that decision has to be made and leads to other paths being followed

Input / output
Shows something added or taken away from process

Terminal / interrupt
Delay, halt or interruption in process

Fig. 5.40

Flow charts graphically show the stages or operations involved in a process such as designing and manufacturing a product. The British Standards Institute has a recommended procedure for doing this which is outlined in their booklets *BS4508* and *PP8888/1*. Each stage in the process is shown by a standard symbol which represents the action to be taken. The sequence of actions is linked with a flow line and arrows showing the direction of flow. The main data processing symbols used represent the preparation, process, terminal/interrupt, input/output and decision. These symbols are shown in Fig. 5.40.

Tips for making flow charts

Flow charts should always start at the top or on the left-hand side of the page.

Keep the layout simple, so that it can be followed easily.

To avoid confusion, make sure the flow lines do not cross.

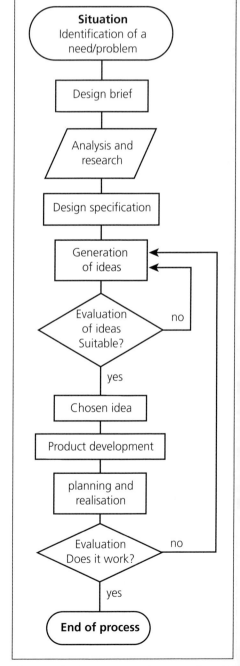

Fig. 5.41 *The design process shown as a flow chart*

Gantt charts

Projects in industry are usually planned using a Gantt chart. They give an overview of what has to happen during the course of the project. This is very important as several things will often be happening at the same time while other tasks will depend on the completion of the previous one.

To make your Gantt chart you must first draw up a table which shows the time-frame that is available to you. This is usually broken down into weeks, or in some cases, into days. On the left side of the chart write down each task. The list of tasks can be taken from those identified by the flow chart headings.

Tasks	Week number																			
	1	2	3	4	5	6	7	8	9	10	11	12	13	14	15	16	17	18	19	20
Situation/identification of a need/problem																				
Design brief																				
Analysis and research																				
Design specification																				
Generation of ideas																				
Evaluation of ideas/Chosen idea																				
Product development																				
Planning and realisation																				
Evaluation																				

Fig. 5.42

Just in time

Just in time is an industrial principle that was developed in Japan to ensure that materials and components required for a project are in the right place at the right time. The overview of the project provided by the Gantt chart tells manufacturers when materials will be needed. A system for ordering can also be built into the schedule to ensure that materials arrive on time. This means that manufacturers do not need to keep stocks of material which take up expensive storage space. Materials arrive when they are required for use. Modern CADCAM systems enable projects to be planned in this way and enable tasks to be carried out simultaneously. This is known as **concurrent engineering**.

Fig. 5.43 *Checking the quality of a print*

Quality control

Quality control is necessary to ensure that all products manufactured and sold are of the best possible quality. Quality control begins with the inspection and testing of the raw materials as they arrive from the suppliers. Quality checks are then made throughout the manufacturing process. The testing of the finished products depends on the scale of production. If the products are being manufactured in large quantities then it will not be possible to test every single product. In this case, samples are taken at regular intervals to monitor the quality of the output.

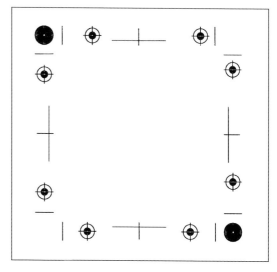

Fig. 5.44 *Registration bars*

Quality control is very important in printing where thousands of copies can be printed in a short time. It is very important in full colour printing that each coloured layer is correctly aligned or registered. Registration marks are printed for each separate plate and the printer has to align the marks carefully before continuing the print run. Colour bars are also used to check the density and colour of the ink.

Fig. 5,45 *Colour bars*

Putting it into practice

1 Draw a block diagram to show the three parts of a system.

2 Explain what is meant by the term *feedback*.

3 Draw a system block diagram for each of the following items:

   a) a personal CD player,

   b) a computer controlled vinyl sign cutter,

   c) a rotary paper trimmer.

4 List four different types of motion and give one example of each.

5 Draw 5 different applications of levers.

6 What is meant by the term *mechanical advantage*?

7 Sketch a mechanism which will reverse linear motion or force.

8 Sketch a mechanism which will transfer rotary motion through 90°.

9 Name three different types of rotary cam.

10 Make a drawing to show how rotary cams convert rotary motion to reciprocating motion.

11 Using notes and sketches, explain how gears can be used to reverse rotary motion.

12 Design a piece of fold-flat advertising to promote a local company.

13 Design a birthday card with a pop-up greeting inside.

14 Draw a circuit diagram for a badge fitted with two flashing LEDs.

15 Draw an LED and explain how it works.

16 Draw the standard symbols for the following electronic components:

   a) a buzzer,

   b) a fixed resistor

   c) a push to make switch.

17 Draw a flow chart for making a hot drink of your choice.

18 Explain how Gantt charts are used in industry and D&T projects.

19 Explain what is meant by the term *just in time*, and describe its advantages.

20 Why is quality control important in industry?

6· Products and applications

Originally, products were designed to fulfil human needs. For example, primitive people made weapons and traps in order to hunt animals for food and skins. Today most products begin their lives as the result of a company's need to capture a larger share of the market and remain competitive. A successful product is now one which improves the quality of life for the consumers and increases wealth for the business.

Fig. 6.1

Needs

As human beings our needs can be quite complex. We all have **basic needs** such as air, water, food, warmth and shelter, but in addition to these, we also have 1 such as the need to be loved, feel wanted and be part of the community. Human needs also vary from one person to another. We may have a need associated with the job we do or the situation we find ourselves in. People with disabilities often have a whole range of special needs which vary according to their disability. Needs also change as people get older. The needs of babies are very different from those of teenagers. Needs associated with our lifestyle or our working practices are referred to as

our **functional needs**. As designers, we have to understand consumers and their needs, both emotional and functional.

In the 1980s the English designer and entrepreneur, Sir Clive Sinclair, designed the C5, a battery powered, pedal assisted tricycle which fulfilled a **functional need** by providing cheap personal transport. However, it failed to meet the **emotional needs** of the users because many of them felt unsafe in the vehicle and it therefore failed to sell in anything like the numbers that Sinclair anticipated.

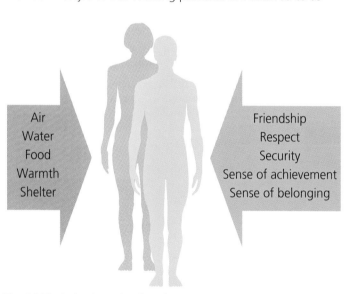

Air	Friendship
Water	Respect
Food	Security
Warmth	Sense of achievement
Shelter	Sense of belonging

Fig. 6.2 *Physical and emotional needs*

Fig. 6.3 *The Sinclair C5*

Fig. 6.4 *Wants or needs?*

Wants

How many times have you said to yourself that you need a new pair of training shoes, or some other fashion item? Do your really need your favourite band's latest CD? It is very easy to confuse wants with needs. What might be seen in Western Europe as a necessity might be seen as a luxury in other parts of the world. The needs of people in developing countries are more likely to be for food, shelter and safety. Designers can create a need using marketing and advertising. Clever marketing techniques can make you feel that you cannot live without a certain product. How often have you seen a TV advert for a product and thought that you **must** have one?

PRODUCT DESIGN

In countries of the developed world, most product design is driven by finance. It usually happens as a response to the need for industry to reduce costs and make greater profits. Product design is carried out to keep ahead of rival companies or competitors in order to secure a larger share of the market or to update an existing product and include new technology.

The product design cycle

Modern manufacturing industries employ market researchers to identify consumer needs and consumer reaction to existing products. This information is then used by the designers to develop new products or update and modify existing ones.

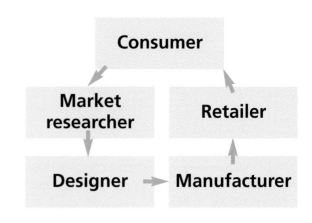

Fig. 6.5 *The product design cycle*

Market research

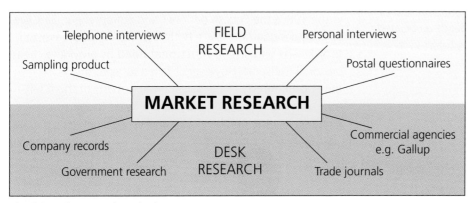

Fig. 6.6 *Market research methods*

There are two aims in market research – to find out the **demand** for a product and to find out **what will make the consumer buy them**. There are a number of different methods of market research (Fig. 6.6). **Field research** involves gaining first-hand information by interviewing people. **Desk research** is about using data that already exists such as official government research or trade reports.

Consumer pull

If a product is to be successful, there must be demand for it. When products are produced in response to an immediate demand it is referred to as consumer pull or demand pull. As long as there is a demand for products from consumers, new and improved products will be designed. Consumers constantly demand better products at lower prices.

Technology push

Products are constantly being redesigned and updated to incorporate new technology. This can be seen in many products used in the home. They are also redesigned to take advantage of new manufacturing technology. CADCAM has been responsible for reducing the time new products take to reach the market place, providing the consumer with greater choice.

Fig. 6.7 *Products developed as a result of consumer pull or technological push*

Research and development

In order to continue to be successful, companies need to develop new products as well as improving old ones. This is usually the responsibility of the marketing department, but larger companies may have a research and development department. Some companies have a new products division which specialises in using information provided by market research along with new technology, where necessary, to design and develop new products.

Protecting designs

In Britain, products, ideas, logos and trademarks can be protected from being copied by applying to the government's Patent Office. The idea of protecting a design dates back to the reign of Henry VIII when a process for making stained glass was protected. **Patents** and copyrights grew out of this and then in 1988 the Patents Act introduced further ways of protecting designs. Patents protect the idea but not the product. They last for 25 years and cannot be renewed. **Registered** designs protects the appearance of a product but not the idea. This is a fairly expensive procedure but it protects new products for up to 25 years. **Copyright** is used to protect works of art, music, literature, typefaces and computer software. Copyright lasts for 70 years after the death of the artist or designer unless the product has been industrially produced, in which case it lasts for 25 years. **Design Right** is an intellectual property right which protects the shape or configuration of the product from being copied for 10 years after it is first marketed.

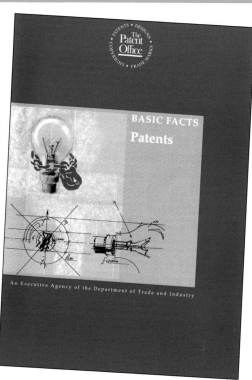

Fig. 6.8 *A wide range of information regarding protecting designs is available from the Patents Office*

The lifecycle of a product

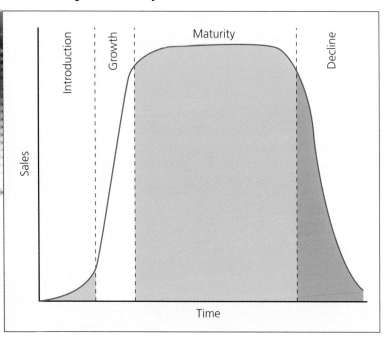

Fig. 6.9 *Graph showing the lifecycle of a product*

Fashion trends and consumers' tastes are constantly changing. Designers and manufacturers must be aware of these changes if they are to remain competitive and keep their share of the market. When new products come onto the market they affect the sales of existing ones. Every product has a life span during which demand for the product changes. The introduction of a new product is expensive as it has to be promoted through marketing and advertising. Until the product has been on sale for a while, the company is unlikely to make much profit. As people get to know about the product the sales increase and less money needs to be spent on marketing. Eventually sales reach a peak and the product sells well. Eventually sales will level off and then begin to decline. This may indicate that the time for updating or restyling the product has come. It may be that the company also decides to incorporate new technology into the manufacturing process at this point or that it is not worth continuing to manufacture the product.

Planned obsolescence

Products are not intended to last for ever. In many cases they are designed to last for only a limited time. Some products like motor cars are designed to last only for a certain number of years. Most graphic products are intended to have a very short life span. Packaging, for example is only required to last until the product arrives at its place of use. Promotional material is only needed for the duration of the advertising or marketing campaign. When considering the life span of their products, designers and manufacturers must also consider waste disposal and recycling. This has an effect on the type of materials that can be used. It is irresponsible to use materials which cannot be recycled or disposed of without harming the environment.

INVESTIGATING EXISTING PRODUCTS

Designers can learn a lot by looking at existing products. It helps them to see how they can improve their own products. You are also likely to be asked to do this as part of your GCSE project work. In order to do this successfully, you will need to draw up a list of criteria to judge the quality of the products. This will have to include meeting the needs, fitness-for-purpose and use of materials. It may be possible for you to use the design specification that you have drawn up for your own project to do this or you may need to look at specific criteria for individual products.

Evaluating existing products

Once you have drawn up a list of criteria, you can use it to evaluate existing products. Use the list of criteria in Fig. 6.10 to evaluate a range of similar products and decide which one is most suitable.

Value analysis

A technique known as value analysis was developed during the Second World War and applied to products by teams of designers and engineers manufacturing armaments (weapons). It is still employed today. Value analysis is the systematic investigation of a product and its manufacture to reduce cost and improve value. It is ususally carried out on products which are manufactured in high volume as they usually have greater potential for savings to be made.

Function
What is the purpose of the product?
What does it have to do?
Is the product fit for the purpose it was designed for?

Market
Who is the customer?
Who is the user?
What are the user's needs likely to be?

Ergonomics
Where is the product used?
Is it comfortable to use?

Aesthetics
Is the product pleasing to look at?
Is it well finished?

Materials and Manufacture
Have the most suitable materials been used?
How has it been manufactured?
Which production process was used: one-off, batch or mass production?

Product life span
How long is the product expected to last?

Quality
Could the quality of the design or the quality of the manufacture be improved?

Safety
Is the product safe to use?
Are there any sharp edges or loose parts?
Do the materials or the manufacturing processes harm the environment?

Costs
How does the cost compare with similar products?

Fig. 6.10 *Product evaluation criteria*

Performance–cost comparison

It is possible to obtain details of the performance of a group of products from the product specifications and compare these with the costs. The data can be shown on a graph like the one in Fig. 6.11. This graph gives an idea of the performance of a range of digital cameras by comparing the size of the CCD (the electronic device which captures the digital image) with the price of the cameras.

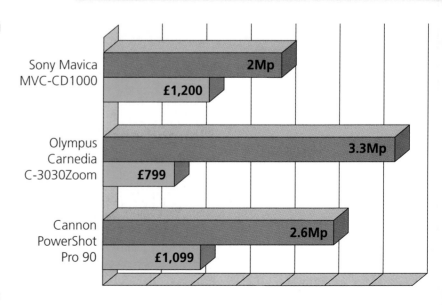

Fig. 6.11 *Performance–cost comparison graph*

Take a closer look at a graphic product

The photographs on this page show the packaging for a chocolate Easter egg. The package design has been printed onto card using the off-set litho process. The window in the front of the box has been die-cut.

This symbol shows that both the *Nestle* and the *KitKat* logos are registered trademarks

The chocolate egg and the chocolate bars are held securely in a vacuum-formed thermoplastic tray.

The development of the box has been taken apart to show the glue tabs

Die-cut window

Bar code

Nutritional values and ingredients

Product information etc.

Fig. 6.12

A close-up of the glue tab shows the colour bar which the printer used to check the ink colour during the quality control process.

Task

Study this product carefully and then evaluate it using the criteria in Fig. 6.10 on page 114.

115

ENVIRONMENTAL ISSUES

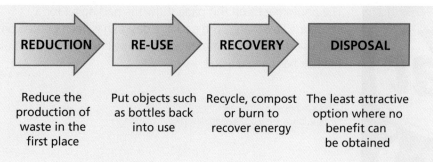

REDUCTION → RE-USE → RECOVERY → DISPOSAL

Reduce the production of waste in the first place

Put objects such as bottles back into use

Recycle, compost or burn to recover energy

The least attractive option where no benefit can be obtained

It is the responsibility of all designers to ensure that their products do as little damage to the environment as possible. Waste should be minimised, products re-used or recycled and, wherever possible, recycled materials should be used in the manufacturing process.

Fig. 6.13 *A waste strategy*

Life cycle analysis

Life cycle analysis (LCA) is a recent development aimed at reducing waste from manufactured products and the processes used to make them. Manufacturers are able to quantify how much energy and raw materials are used and how much solid, liquid and gaseous waste is generated at each stage. The resulting data is an indication to the manufacturer of the impact their product will have on the environment.

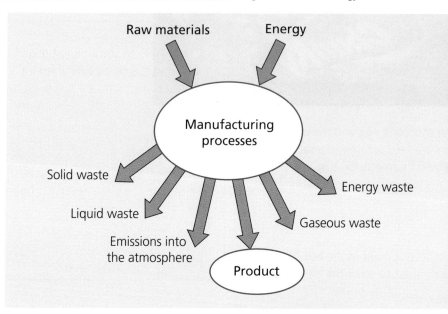

Raw materials · Energy · Manufacturing processes · Solid waste · Liquid waste · Emissions into the atmosphere · Product · Gaseous waste · Energy waste

Fig. 6.14 *Life cycle analysis*

Graphic products can be produced quite easily using recycled or recyclable materials. As a designer, it is important that you reduce the amount of materials used as far as possible, especially in packaging projects that are thrown away immediately after use. Graphic products are also used to inform people of environmental issues. The following example shows how graphic products can be used in a major project to reassure people with environmental concerns.

Fig. 6.15

The Burton Waters project

BURTON WATERS

PROPOSALS AND DEVELOPMENT CONSIDERATIONS

Fig. 6.16

Burton waters is a major environmental design project that involves changing the use of 137 acres of riverside land to create a marina, lakes and parkland, along with associated facilities such as parking, restaurants and shops. It is, therefore, a large and very expensive project. It is being financed by a number of business people and organisations.

Not surprisingly, local people and groups, who have a particular concern for environmental issues, wanted to be assured that the project would be an improvement to the area and would not harm the existing natural environment.

The architectural design company Costall Allen Design were commissioned to both design the development and to present the environmental case for it. They produced a very detailed report and environmental statement, as well as a scale model of the complete project.

The report and environmental statement

The logo used for this project was designed to show human leisure pursuits, represented by sailing, in harmony with the natural habitat, represented by birds and fishes. It is shown below in detail, and can be seen on each page of the report. Other interesting design features of the report to note include the use of a water image, rectangular shaped shades of subtle colours and simple line drawings.

Below you can see a typical page from the report. It shows some interesting aspects of layout. White space has been used to good effect, and the text is in a two-column format which makes it easier to read. The line drawings of the boats and quayside show the designers' ideas of what part of the finished development might look like. The drawings were made using a pencil, and the colour shades were added during the printing process. The pages are numbered, and each displays both the project logo and the designers' logo.

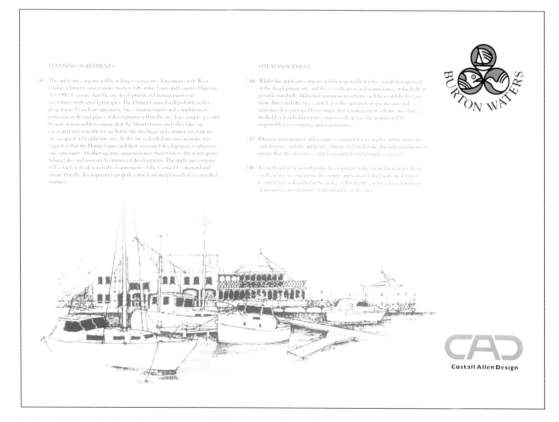

It is useful to look at documents of this type to learn about style. This report is an A3-size folder with a card front and back, and a ring-type binder similar to that used on many design technology projects. Could some aspects of this style be used to improve the presentation of your project folders?

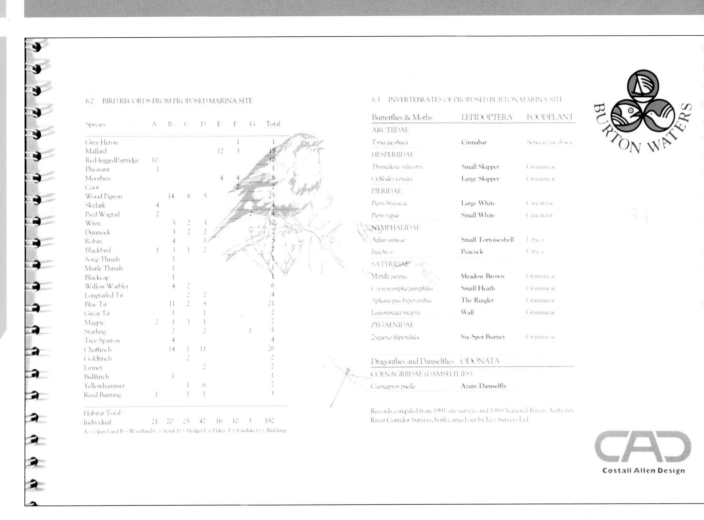

6.2 BIRD RECORDS FROM PROPOSED MARINA SITE

Species	A	B	C	D	E	F	G	Total
Grey Heron						1		1
Mallard					12	3		15
Red-legged Partridge	10							10
Pheasant	1							1
Moorhen					4	4		8
Coot					2			2
Wood Pigeon		14	6	5				25
Skylark	4							4
Pied Wagtail	2							4
Wren		5	2	3				10
Dunnock		3	2	2				7
Robin		4		1				5
Blackbird	1	3	1	2				7
Song Thrush		1						1
Mistle Thrush		1						1
Blackcap		1						1
Willow Warbler	4	2						6
Longtailed Tit			2	2				4
Blue Tit		11	2	8				21
Great Tit		1		1				2
Magpie	2	1	3	1				7
Starling		2		2		1		5
Tree Sparrow	4							4
Chaffinch		14	1	11				26
Goldfinch		2						2
Linnet				2				2
Bullfinch		1						1
Yellowhammer			1	6				7
Reed Bunting	1		1	1				3
Habitat Total:								
Individual	21	70	25	47	16	10	3	192

A = Open Land B = Woodland C = Scrub D = Hedges E = Dykes F = Fosdyke G = Buildings

6.3 INVERTEBRATES OF PROPOSED BURTON MARINA SITE

Butterflies & Moths	LEPIDOPTERA	FOODPLANT
ARCTIIDAE		
Tyria jacobaea	Cinnabar	Senecio jacobaea
HESPERIIDAE		
Thymelicus sylvestris	Small Skipper	Gramineae
Ochlodes venata	Large Skipper	Gramineae
PIERIDAE		
Pieris brassicae	Large White	Cruciferae
Pieris rapae	Small White	Cruciferae
NYMPHALIDAE		
Aglais urticae	Small Tortoiseshell	Urtica
Inachis io	Peacock	Urtica
SATYRIDAE		
Maniola jurtina	Meadow Brown	Gramineae
Coenonympha pamphilus	Small Heath	Gramineae
Aphantopus hyperanthus	The Ringlet	Gramineae
Lasiommata megera	Wall	Gramineae
ZYGAENIDAE		
Zygaena filipendulae	Six-Spot Burnet	Gramineae

Dragonflies and Damselflies	ODONATA	
COENAGRIIDAE (DAMSELFLIES)		
Coenagrion puella	Azure Damselfly	

Records compiled from 1991 site surveys and 1989 National Rivers Authority River Corridor Surveys, both carried out by Eco Surveys Ltd.

The report contains data about the current inhabitants of the area that has been collected over a period of time. Such research is necessary to ensure that the development does not upset the balance of nature, and that the correct type of natural habitat is preserved. It is often difficult to present tables of data in an interesting format. Here, in an effort to enhance the presentation, the designers have used another line drawing, this time set behind the text.

This is a page that has been made up from a portion of an Ordnance Survey map. Details have been added to show the location of the development. The right-hand portion has been 'faded out' so that the logos and page number can be inserted to retain the overall style of the report. When parts of maps are copied, the publishers of the document have to get permission from the copyright owners, in this case, HMSO (Her Majesty's Stationery Office).

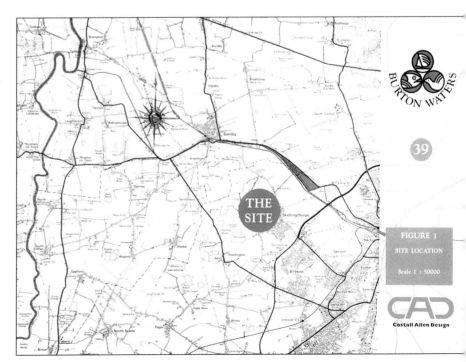

FIGURE 1
SITE LOCATION
Scale 1 : 50000

Maps and models

The map on the right is another location map. This one has been simplified in order to pick out only the detail that the designer wants to draw attention to. It shows where the development will be located in relation to the nearest town, nearby villages, major roads, the Fossdyke Navigation (the Fossdyke is a canal built by the Romans to link the rivers Witham and Trent) and the railway line.

The map below is the designers' plan of the site. Notice how it has been sensitively coloured using pencil crayons over a textured surface (see page 49). Also, colour has been added to the line drawings. Such drawings of completed projects are often referred to as 'artist's impressions'. They are made to make the completed development look its best, in this case with boats and attractive buildings.

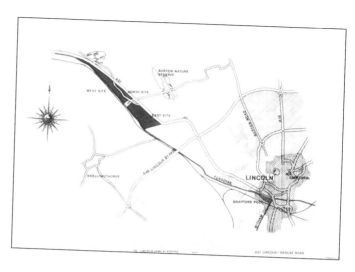

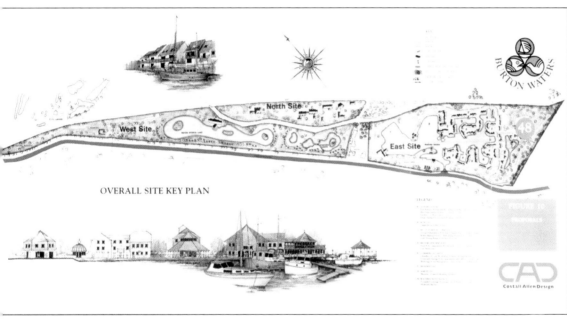

OVERALL SITE KEY PLAN

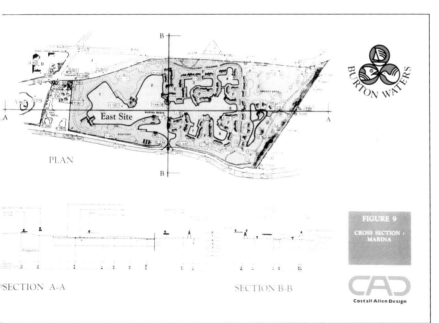

PLAN

SECTION A-A   SECTION B-B

Environmental design

The map on the left shows two sectional views through the actual marina part of the development. They indicate the depth of the water and the access to the marina for boats from the Fossdyke Navigation. The sectional views also show the flood defences.

119

The main means of communicating the design for Burton Waters was through the medium of a scale model. The model was produced to a scale of 1:1000, and even then it is 2.9 metres long! In the photograph on the left you can see members of the design team discussing aspects of the project.

The model has been made from a whole range of modelling media, including wood, paper, card, plastic sheet and plaster of Paris (see modelling materials on pages 88–89). If you look very carefully at the close-up photographs of the model shown here, you will see a small error – the masts of the sail boats are too long to fit under the footbridges. Even professional model makers sometimes make mistakes!

The model for Burton Waters turned out to be so impressive that it now stands on display in the entrance foyer of the developer's offices.

Burton Waters Today

The Burton Waters development is progressing extremely well with approximately half of the waterside properties sold. The Boatyard, Chandlery, Boat Workshop and the Burton Waters Management Centre are now open with CCTV operational on over 50% of the site. Burton Waters Health, Leisure & Racquet Club has opened and now has over 4,000 members.

The fishing lakes are complete and stocked with fish. The leisure lake has been excavated and water allowed to fill the area.

Major structural landscaping and land modelling is being undertaken, including the planting of 100,000 bulbs such as bluebells and snowdrops. A substantial amount of car parking has been constructed. Users and operators for lake side cottages, hotel and conference centre, food and drink operations and small retail shop and office units, are being sought. The aim is to have the development fully completed by the end of 2005.

The illustrations shown here are taken from the graphic designer's sketches and drawings for this project.

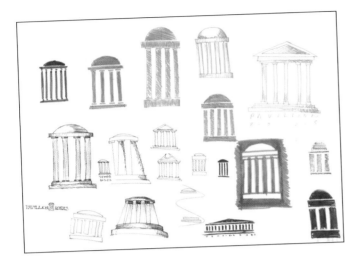

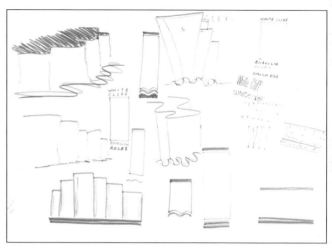

Company name

The designer's first task was to suggest suitable names for the subsidiary company. The English nature of the rose was taken as a theme and various possibilities were explored before deciding on 'The English Rose Company'.

The sketches shown on the right illustrate some of the initial ideas for getting across a feeling of 'Englishness'. They have been very quickly drawn using marker and fine line pens.

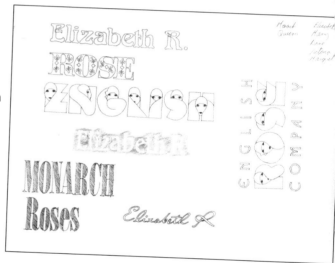

Logo design

Once a company name had been established, the next task was to design a logo. The inspiration for this came from a traditional playing card design. The sketches on the right show how the idea for the company logo was developed from this starting point. The idea for a crown above the logo came from English hallmarks. These are the marks which are stamped on to silver and gold to indicate the purity of the metal, the makers of the object, and the year it was made.

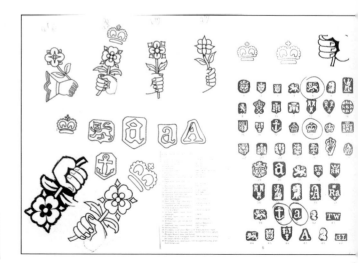

Developing ideas

The sketches on this page show how the designer developed the original idea and the hallmark theme into a suitable design which has an 'English' feel to it.

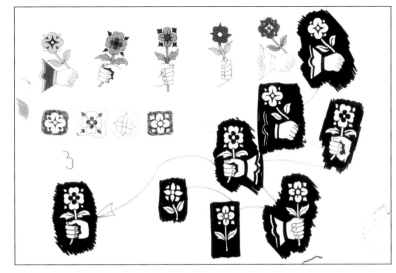

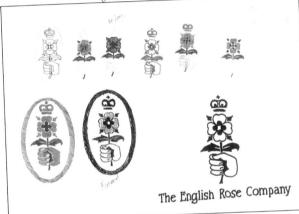

Marker pen has been used to highlight around the ideas. This makes the ideas stand out and also creates a more realistic 'hallmarked' image.

The drawings on the left show how the designer has experimented with typefaces and lettering. Again, the aim here was to maintain the traditional 'English' theme.

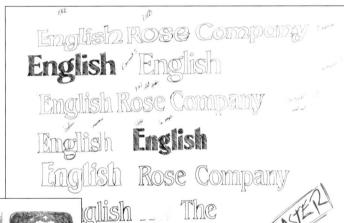

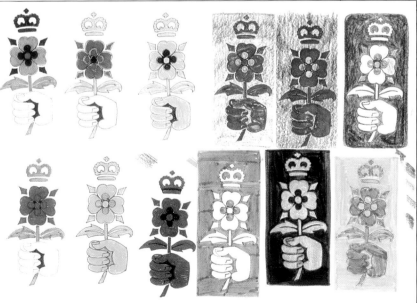

The illustration below shows how the designer considered colour coordination. Coloured pencil and marker pen has been used to explore possible colour combinations. Along the edge, you can see where the designer has begun to match them to Pantone colours.

123

Corporate image design

These illustrations show how the designer arrived at the final logo design. Notice that the rectangular 'hallmark' background of the logo has been changed in favour of a softer, more classic elliptical design. The name of the company has also been shortened, to 'English Rose Company'.

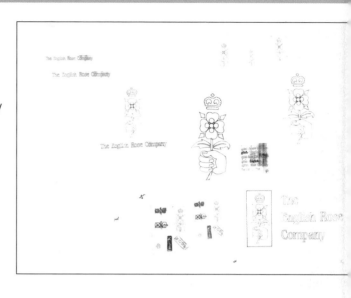

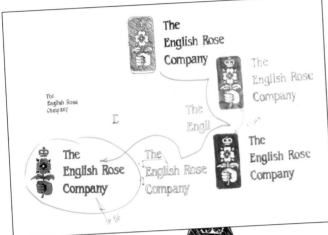

The final artwork for the logo is shown on the left. This will be photographed so that a printing plate can be made from it. Notice the registration marks on the artwork. These will be used by the printer to accurately align the work when printing. They are very important when printing in more than one colour so that each colour fits together perfectly.

124

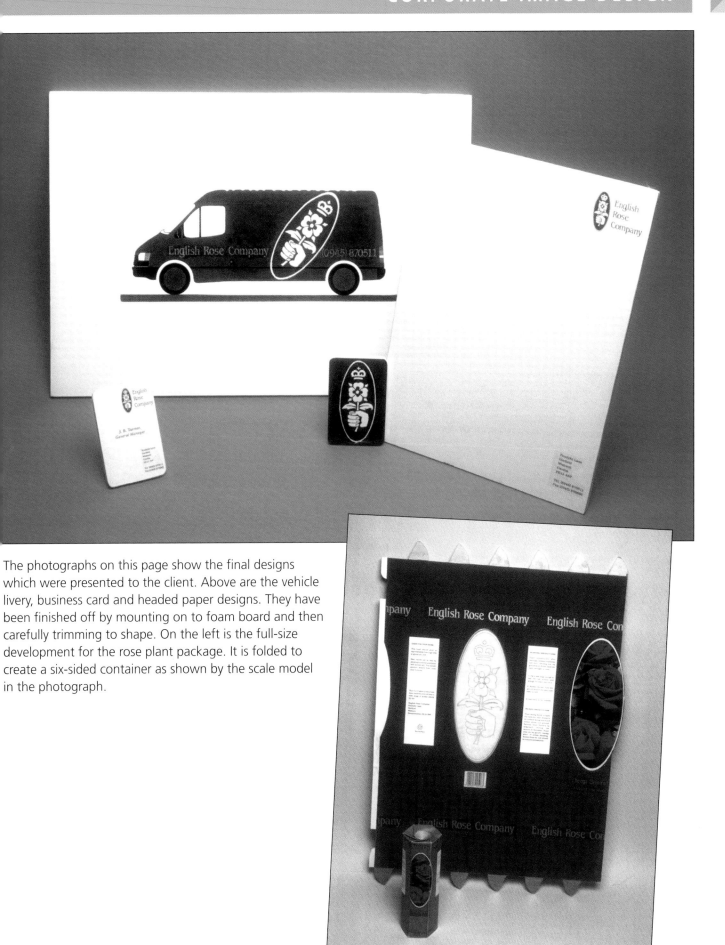

The photographs on this page show the final designs which were presented to the client. Above are the vehicle livery, business card and headed paper designs. They have been finished off by mounting on to foam board and then carefully trimming to shape. On the left is the full-size development for the rose plant package. It is folded to create a six-sided container as shown by the scale model in the photograph.

Acknowledgements

The publishers would like to thank the following:

For their help in providing case study material:
Aesseal plc; Alan Miller Bunford; Barking Dog Art; Sanford UK; Burton Waters; CAD Associates; Castle Customs; Colin Plant, Graphic Designer; English Rose Company; Griffen Paper Mill; LINPAC

For permission to reproduce photographs and illustrations:
Ace Photo Library (fig 1.29 and 2.129); AKG London (Page 5 Middle left and bottom left); Benedicta Nakawuki (fig. 2.117); Berol (fig 2.60 top and 2.68); BSI (fig 3.29, 3.35, and 3.39); Casey Rutland (fig 2.75); Caterpillar (fig 1.23); CBI statistics graph:source ONS Index of production (fig 1.9); Collins Educational (fig 1.26, fig 4.1); Colin Chapman (fig 2.71); Colin Plant (fig 2.2 and 2.64); Corbis (page 5 top right; 1.10, 1.11, 1.12, 1.28, 2.112, 2.114, 2.115, 4.2, 4.3); Crocodile Clips (fig 5.24); Daily Telegraph (fig 2.31); Daler Rowney (fig 2.106); Digital Photo User (fig 6.11); EMA Model Supplies (fig 4.4 and 4.6); European Gas Turbines (page 66 top); Graeme Morris (fig 5.3); HarperCollins Publishers (fig 5.17); Haynes Publishers (fig 3.40); Imagelink (page 21 top left); John Frost Newspapers (fig 1.5); Ken Vail Graphic Design (fig 2.126); Kit Kat (fig. 6.12); Landrover (fig 3.51); Letraset UK Ltd (fig 2.86); London Aerial Photography (fig 1.7 and 1.9); MG Rover (fig 3.48); Microsoft Corporation (fig 1.30); Middlesex University Teaching Resources (fig 4.17, 4.18 and 4.19); Mike Finney (fig 2.32); Patents Office (fig 6.8); Pat Winter, HarperCollins Publishers (figs 1.14, fig 2.13); Peter Gould (fig 1.4, 3.22, 5.21); Peter Morris (page 5 bottom centre; fig 3.8, 4.11, 4.12, 4.13, 4.44, 5.44, 5.45, 6.4); Popperfoto (fig 1.226); Rebecca Capper (fig. 2.70); Roland Digital (fig 3.20 and 3.21); Science Photo Library (fig. 1.3, 1.18, 1.19,1.37, 2.47, 3.18, 4.3, 5.14, 5.43, 6.1, 6.7); Sinclair (fig 2.104); Sittingbourne Paper Company (page 23 top); Techsoft UK Ltd (fig. 2.125, 2.130, 2.131, 2.132, 2.133, 3.15, 4.39); Tom Morgan 2.60 bottom, 2.65, 2.66, 2.68 and 2.69); Tracktronics (fig 5.25): Trip (fig 1.141, 1.42, 1.44, 2.104, 2.106, 3.3); Walton Designs (fig 4.4 and 4.6); Warwick Manufacturing Group (fig 4.8 and 4.10); Zefa (fig 2.47)

Published by HarperCollins*Publishers* Limited

77–85 Fulham Palace Road
Hammersmith
London
W6 8JB

www.CollinsEducation.com
Online support for schools and colleges

© HarperCollins*Publishers* Limited 2002
First published 2002

ISBN 0 00 711531 8

Mike Finney asserts the moral right to be identified as the author of this work.

All rights reserved. No part of this publication may be reproduced, stored in a retrieval system, or transmitted in any form or by any means, electronic, mechanical, photocopying, recording or otherwise, without either the prior permission of the Publisher or a licence permitting restricted copying in the United Kingdom issued by the Copyright Licensing Agency Ltd., 90 Tottenham Court Road, London W1P 0LP.

British Library Cataloguing in Publication Data
A catalogue record for this publication is available from the British Library

Designed by Ken Vail Graphic Design, Cambridge
Cover photograph by Tony Stone Images
Commissioning Editor: Martin Davies
Project Editor: Benedicta Nakawuki

Other useful texts
Real World Technology Series
Resistant Materials
Electronic Products
Food Technology

Index

A

abbreviations 79
ABS 16, 89, 95
accessories for modelling 98
acrylic 88, 94, 95, 99
acrylic paints 41, 99
adhesives 59, 99
Adobe software 57, 60, 61
advertising 11, 104
aerospace industry 8
AESSEAL plc 66–73
airbrushing 54–5
angles 66, 80, 81
applications and products 111–25
architectural drawings 10, 29, 35
armatures 96
artist's impressions 119
assembly drawings 78
AutoCAD 70
automotive industry 8

B

backgrounds 58
ball pens 25
Barking Dog Art 44–7
batch production 9
Berol 24–5
biotechnology industry 8
bisecting angles and lines 81
bitmaps 63
bleed-proof paper 50
blending 52
blow moulding 17
boards, choice of 22–3
British Standards Institution
   see BSI
brushes 45
BSI 68, 73, 79
   BS308 69, 72
   BS4508 108
bulbs, electrical 107
Burton Waters project 116–21
buzzers 107

C

CADCAM 60, 62, 67–72, 97
   CAD 10, 65, 68, 92, 106
cameras 56–7
cams 103
card 62, 88, 91, 99
cartridge paper 23, 65
Castle Customs 60–3
chalk, paper for 23
charcoal 24
chroma 36
CIM (computer integrated
   manufacture) 10
circles 27, 33, 34, 67, 80
   and curved surfaces 93
circuit boards 106
circuits 106
clay 96
cleaning equipment 67

client approval 13
clipart 60
clutch pencils 24
CMYK 15
CNC machine tools 72
colour 36–9, 43
   colour printing 15, 109
colour wheel 37
coloured pencils 40, 46, 48, 50
   for presentation drawings 53
commissioning 13
compass cutters 91
compasses 67
components 98, 107
computers see CADCAM; ICT
consumer pull 112
continuous production 9
contrast, colour 38
control
   and planning 101, 108–9
   and systems 101–10
conventions on drawings 79
copyright 113
CorelDRAW 61
corporate image design 122–5
corriflute 89
CAD Associates 30–3
costings 13
costs 114
craft knives 91
crating 29, 33
Crocodile Technology 106
curves 33, 66, 93
cutters 61, 87, 91, 92
   for vinyl 62, 63, 99
cutting mats 91

D

demand 112
demonstration models 86
desert landscape 48
design 10, 13, 108
   corporate image design 122–5
   environmental design 116–21
   product design 112–13
   protecting 113
   see also CADCAM
Design tools, Techsoft 62, 63
designers, graphic 13, 36–9
desktop publishing (DTP) 13, 60
development, research and 112
developments 62, 91, 92–3
digital cameras 56, 57
dimensioning drawings 68, 70
dip pens 44
dividing a line 81
drawing
   3-dimensional drawing 28–33
   freehand sketching 26–7
   geometrical drawing 65, 80–3
   instruments and equipment
   65–7
   materials for 22–5

technical drawing 10, 65–79
   see also sketching
drawing boards 65
drawings
   architectural drawings 10, 29, 35
   assembly drawings 78
   for communication 10
   conventions on 79
   isometric drawings 28
   oblique drawings 28
   planometric drawings 29
   presentation drawings 10, 53,
   58–9
   rendering 46–9, 50
   standardising 72–3
dry media 40
dry mounting 59
DTP (desktop publishing) 13, 60

E

EasiCAD 70
economy, the 7, 8
electronic components 107
electronic systems 106
ellipses 27, 83
engineering drawing 10
English Rose Company 122–5
environmental issues 116–21
equipment and tools 22, 65–7, 91

F

fabric, adhesives for 99
fabricating models 91
feedback 101
felt-tipped pens 40
film, photographic 56
fine-lead pencils 24
finishing models 99
first angle projection 75–6
fixative sprays 24, 40
floating layers 105
flow charts 10, 108
foam 97, 99
foam board 89, 99
fold-flat advertising 104
food industry 8
form, shape and 34–5, 36
forming 16, 94–5
four-colour process printing 15
freehand sketching 26–7

G

Gantt charts 109
GDP 8
gears 103
geometrical drawing 65, 80–3
geometry 65, 80–3, 92–3
glass, rendering 47
gouache 22, 23, 41, 54
graphic designers 13, 36–9
graphic products 11, 12, 13
   manufacturing 14–17
   mechanisms in 104–5
graphics industry 12–13

graphics in manufacturing 10–11
graphics techniques 21–64
Griffen Paper Mill 22–3
Gross Domestic Product 8

H

hard copy 71
harmony, colour 36–7, 38
highlighter pens 43
highlighting ideas 42–3
highlights in rendering 47, 48, 50
hue 36

I

ICT (information and
   communication technology) 10,
   60–3
   for artwork 13, 44, 45
   in circuit design 106
   in modelling 87, 92, 97, 99
   and photographic images 13,
   56–7
   for technical drawing 65, 70–1
   see also CADCAM
Illustrator, Adobe 61
image manipulation 57
Industrial Revolution 6
industry 6–11
   graphics industry 12–13
   safety in 18–19
information and communication
   technology see ICT
injection moulding 17
inks 22, 23, 44–5
   airbrushing 54
   printing with 14, 15
   weighted line with 42
input 101, 102, 103, 106, 108
inputting information 71
instant cameras 56
instruments, drawing 65–7
   see also tools
interaction, colour 38
isometric drawings 28

J

jobbing production 9
JPEG files 13, 56, 57, 60
just in time 109

K

kits, modelling with 98
knives 25, 91

L

laminating 59
layout, drawing 72
LDRs 107
LEDs 107
lenticular sheet 90
levers 102
libraries, artwork 60
life cycle analysis 116
life cycle, product 113

Peters

Index

light 35, 36
line bending 94
lines 42, 68, 80, 81
linkages 103
LINPAC 92–3
liquid crystals 90
logos, designing 122–4

M

manufacturing industry 6–8, 9
  graphics in 10–11
manufacturing processes 14–17
maps 118–19
markers 22, 40, 44, 50–3
market research 112
marketing 11
masking 52, 55
mass production 9
materials 22–5
  for modelling 88
  plastic *see* plastic materials
  smart materials 90
MDF 16, 89, 99
mechanical advantage 102
mechanical systems 102–3
mechanisms 104–5
media 22, 40–1
  for airbrushing 54
metals 48, 50, 89, 90, 99
Microsoft software 60, 61
modelling 85–100
  3D solid modelling 70–1
  circuits 106
modelling foam 97
modelling wax 97
models 85–6
  Burton Waters case study 120
motion 102
motors 107
moulding 17, 96–7
moulds for vacuum forming 95
mounting drawings 58–9
multiple layers 105

N

names, company, choosing 122
needs and wants 111

O

oblique drawings 28
obsolescence, planned 113
offset lithography 14
one-off production 9
opaque plastic, rendering 47
orthographic projection 74–7, 78
output 101, 102, 103, 106, 108
output devices 107

P

packaging 11, 61, 62, 92–3
PageMaker, Adobe 60
paint 23, 41, 46
Paint Shop Pro 57
paper 22–3, 41, 50

adhesives for 99
  for modelling 88
papier-mâché 96
parallel motion 65
paste up 13
pastels 40, 46, 48
patents 113
pencils 22, 23, 24–5
  coloured 40, 46, 48, 50, 53
  in technical drawing 68, 76
  weighted line with 42
pens 23, 25, 44, 68
  felt-tipped pens 40
  highlighter pens 43
  technical pens 44, 50
perception, colour 39
perforating tools 91
performance-cost comparison 114
perpendiculars, constructing 81
perspective 28, 30–1, 32, 35
pharmaceutical industry 8
photography 56–7
PhotoShop, Adobe 57
plane geometry 80–3
planned obsolescence 113
planning and control 101, 108–9
planometric drawings 29
plans, production 10
plastic materials 16–17, 94–5
  for modelling 88–9, 90
  rendering 47, 50
plasticard 89
plasticine 96
polished surfaces 47, 48
polyethylene (polythene) 17, 95
polygons 80, 82
polymer clays 96
polymorph 90
polypropylene sheet 90
polystyrene 16, 88, 89, 95, 97
  adhesives for 99
pop-ups 105
PP7307 108
PP7308 69, 72
presentation drawings 10, 53,
  58–9
presentation models 86
press bending 94
primary colours 37
printing 14–15, 109
process 101, 106, 108
process production 9
ProDesktop 65, 70, 87
product design 112–13
product safety 18
production 13
  scale of 9
products 111–25
  investigating existing 114
  lifecycle 113
ProENGINEER 70
projection, orthographic 74–7
proof copy 13

protecting designs 113
protecting work 59
prototype models 85
prototyping 87
protractors 66
Publisher, Microsoft 60

Q

quadrilaterals, drawing 80
quality control 109
QuarkXpress 60

R

rapid prototyping 87
reflective surfaces 47, 48
registered designs 113
rendering 46–9, 50
research and development 112
resistors 107
retailing 11
rigid foam materials 89, 99
risk assessment 19
Roland Camm cutters 61, 87, 92
  for vinyl 62, 63, 99
rotary cutters 91
roughs 13
rulers, safety 91

S

safety 18–19
safety rulers 91
sales of graphics products 12
Sanford UK 24–5
scale of production 9
scales on drawings 73
scalpels 91
scanning images 57
screen printing 15
secondary colours 37
sections 78
sensors 107
set squares 66
shade 35
shadows 35
shape and form 34–5, 36
shapes, constructing 80, 82–3
SignLab 61, 62, 63
signs 61, 62, 63
simulation, computer 87
single-point perspective 28, 31
sizes, paper 22–3
sketch models 86
sketching 10, 26–7
  see also drawing
smart materials 90
smart wire 90
software *see* ICT
solid geometry 80, 92–3
speakers 107
spraying marker ink 52
  see also airbrushing
stage set design 86–9
standardising drawings 72–3

styrofoam 89, 97, 99
sub-systems 101
support 22
switches 107
systems and control 101–10

T

technical drawing 10, 65–79
technical pens 44, 50
technology industries 8
technology push 112
Techsoft software 61, 62, 63, 92,
  99
templates 67
tertiary colours 37
texture 46–9
  of paper 23
thermistors 107
thermocolour sheet 90
thermoforming 16
thermoplastics 16, 94–5
third angle projection 75, 77
35 mm cameras 56
3-dimensional work
  CAD/CAM systems 68–72
  drawing 28–33, 34
  modelling 85–6
  see also modelling
tone 36, 42, 51
tools and equipment 22, 65–7, 91
tracing paper 65
transducers 107
transferring motion 102, 103
transparent plastic, rendering 47
triangles, drawing 80
2D Designer, Techsoft 61, 92, 99
two-point perspective 32

V

v fold 105
vacuum forming 16, 95
value analysis 114
vanishing points 28, 31, 32–3, 35
vector images 63, 70
video cameras 57
viewpoints 31
vinyl signs 61, 62, 63
virtual prototyping 87

W

wants and needs 111
washes 23, 41, 45
wasting 97
watercolour 22, 23, 41
wax, modelling 97
weight of paper 23
weighted line 42
wet media 22, 41
wheel, colour 37
wood 16, 46, 89, 91, 99
Word, Microsoft 60, 61